# Two Dollar Dinners

# Two Dollar Dinners

Meals and menus for $2

**Paul Gayler**

Photographs by Philip Wilkins

ARTUS BOOKS

LONDON

Artus Books, London

First published in Great Britain in 1996 by
George Weidenfeld & Nicolson Ltd
The Orion Publishing Group
Orion House
5 Upper St Martin's Lane
London WC2H 9EA

British Library Cataloguing-in-Publication Data
A catalogue for this book is available from the British Library.

ISBN 1-898-79953-9

Designed by The Senate
Printed and bound in Italy

# Contents

# INTRODUCTION

The idea behind this book stemmed from a telephone call I received at The Lanesborough Hotel in London one Friday morning in September 1995. Simon Hinde, the Consumer Affairs Correspondent of the English *Sunday Times* called me to ask if I was willing to take up the challenge of devising a three-course menu for a family of four, with a budget of just $2. The idea behind this article, he told me, was to bring to people's attention the growing number of discount stores popping up all over Britain. The same phenomenon has already happened in America, with Sam's Club and Costco selling food which is considerably cheaper than the well-known supermarket chains.

At first I thought the idea was absurd; what meal could possibly be made for $2? However, since my resolve and professionalism had been challenged, I felt that I could not refuse. I set about finding out more. Simon faxed me a list of about 10–12 discount items he had bought, such as cans of beans, plum tomatoes, bread, milk, and sausages. Even so, the saving grace was that I was allowed a basic storecupfull of ingredients that you might find in any home.

My menu, after much thought and toying with prices on my calculator, consisted of spicy Mexican-style soup made from baked beans, followed by fusilli with hot dogs, tomatoes, and herbs and, to finish, cinnamon-infused baked apple. The whole menu was simplicity itself, well flavored and reasonably priced, in fact only $1.50 for three courses. A little chili pepper for the soup, a few dried herbs for the pasta, and cinnamon for the apples had worked wonders. I was pleased with myself, but Simon wanted to put the menu to a further test.

He arranged for a family of four to dine at The Lanesborough to eat my $1.50 meal. The two adults and their two children arrived early one evening at the hotel, a little sceptical of what could be achieved with $2.

After meeting them I returned to the kitchen determined to impress my guests. I'm glad to say the meal proved to be a great success. In fact, they even asked for the soup recipe! The children left their plates clean, and having four children of my own, I know that this can sometimes be an achievement in itself.

The publicity that the article in the following weekend's *Sunday Times* attracted was hard to conceive. It made headlines in both American and Mexican newspapers as well, and I got telephone calls from fellow chefs, readers, and even an Italian TV network.

Three months later I began to create this book on similar lines to my challenge; with the aid of a basic kitchen cupboard, I set out to produce menus that vary from $2 for four to $2 per person. The recipes follow my passion for food from around the world, taking their inspiration from Mexico through Europe to the Far East.

Nowadays, thanks to price wars in all the major food chains, simple but interesting meals are within the grasp of any home cook on a budget. Making the most of seasonal ingredients, the best quality convenience foods, and a little imagination, cheap need never mean boring. Used creatively, herbs, spices, and condiments add flavor to cheaper cuts of meat and fish. Most of the recipes in this book are fairly easy to prepare and incredibly easy on the pocket.

All the recipes are for 4 people unless stated otherwise. I hope that you enjoy trying them.

*Paul*

# THE **KITCHEN CUPBOARD**

Home cooking has changed dramatically over the last decade. A steady stream of television programs celebrating food and foreign travel, backed up by magazine articles and advertisements, has opened our eyes to the many flavors the world has to offer. We also love to eat out and experience new foods at every opportunity. This new-found interest is reflected in the contents of our kitchen cupboards; they are now likely to contain many more unusual ingredients—sauces, spices, herbs, different types of rice and pasta—than they would have done a few years ago.

So, what constitutes the basics of a kitchen cupboard? In a way, it is impossible to summarize, since so much depends on the style of food that you personally enjoy and generally cook at home. However, one thing is for certain: Well-stocked cupboards will open the door to a greater choice of imaginative and exotic meals that the home cook can prepare easily and without further expense.

The following lists constitute what I consider staples of kitchen cupboards (in fact, this is more or less what is in my cupboards at home). All the items are featured in the recipes within this book, some more frequently than others. There's no need to rush out and spend a fortune on stocking up: You will already have many of the ingredients, and others can be bought when you need them.

### Everyday basics

These are found in most households:
Salt, black pepper (preferably in a pepper mill, ready to be freshly ground, giving a far superior flavor to ready-ground pepper), vegetable oil (buy a neutral-flavored oil such as sunflower oil, for sautéing and general use), olive oil (choose extra virgin olive oil for using in dressings and sauces), butter (margarine has its uses, but cannot compare with the flavor of butter), milk (low-fat is healthier than whole milk), eggs, all-purpose, white and brown sugar, bread, tea, coffee.

### Sauces and condiments

These are my favorite flavor enhancers:
Mayonnaise, light soy sauce, ketchup, tomato paste, pesto sauce, Worcestershire sauce, Tabasco sauce, anchovy extract, capers in brine, black olives, white and red wine vinegar, balsamic vinegar, curry paste, mustard, horseradish, tahini paste.

Chicken, vegetable, and beef broth are invaluable in the kitchen. Some supermarkets now sell good-quality ready-made broth, but don't be afraid to use a bouillon cube, as it's fine for many purposes.

### Perishables

Basic vegetables and fruits could include:
Fresh garlic, onions, scallions, carrots, celery, leeks, potatoes, fresh ginger, lemons, oranges.

In the refrigerator you might also keep orange juice, a well-wrapped piece of Parmesan cheese, plain yogurt, and margarine.

Perishable in the sense that it gets eaten as soon as bought, unless well hidden, chocolate is also useful as an ingredient. Buy semi-sweet chocolate.

### Herb and spice rack

Dried herbs are no substitute for fresh. If at all possible, I recommend that you start your own herb garden, which might include parsley, chives, mint, thyme, and sage. The following dried herbs are acceptable if fresh herbs are not available:

Bay leaf, thyme, sage, oregano, rosemary, mixed herbs.

Spices from around the world give dishes hot or subtle flavors and great depth of taste. Most spices tend to lose their flavor very quickly once they have been ground, so it is best to buy whole spices (seeds or pods) and grind them yourself just before using them. Alternatively, buy ground spices in small quantities: This is one occasion when it is a false economy to buy in bulk. I use a lot of spices, and the following are some of my favorites:

Red pepper flakes, cayenne pepper, paprika, coriander seeds, cumin, cinnamon, cardamom, nutmeg, cloves, caraway seeds, allspice, turmeric, ground ginger.

Ready-made spice mixtures, such as mild curry powder and garam masala, are also useful.

Fennel seeds, sesame seeds, and Chinese five-spice powder appear once or twice in this book, and are worth buying if you are particularly fond of Indian or Chinese cooking.

### Not just for cakes

Dried fruit and nuts can also be used in savory dishes, and to add a touch of luxury to simple desserts:

Cornstarch, baking powder, vanilla extract, yeast (I prefer to use compressed yeast, but active dry yeast is easier to keep as a standby; however, don't keep it too long or it may lose its efficacy), raisins, golden raisins, prunes, walnut halves, whole and flaked almonds, sweetened, shredded cocounut.

### Cans

These items can be lifesavers, and can easily be converted into new and exciting dishes:

Plum tomatoes (whole and chopped, in various sizes), baked beans, corn, black beans, cannellini beans, chickpeas, coconut milk, tuna, herrings, sardines, red salmon, anchovy fillets.

### Jars

The sweet-toothed may have these already, but several of them can also be used to create savory dishes:

Good-quality raspberry and apricot jam, redcurrant jelly, orange marmalade, clear honey, maple syrup, peanut butter, molasses.

### Pasta and grains

Dried pasta is always a good kitchen cupboard standby, and other grains also make satisfying meals:

Long, rounded pasta such as spaghetti or linguine; flat noodles such as trenette or tagliatelle; lasagne; small pasta shapes, such as fusilli, penne, rigatoni, macaroni; a selection of different types of rice might include long-grain white rice and brown rice (for salads and general purposes), basmati (a particularly fragrant rice with long thin grains), arborio (a rounded grain rice, used to make risotto); other grains that are good for absorbing sauces include polenta (cornmeal) and couscous.

### Drinks cabinet

I have long been of the opinion that a dish without booze in it, with it, or both is somehow incomplete. One glass for the pot and one for the cook is one of my favorite rules of the kitchen. Joking aside, wines and spirits are invaluable in cooking, especially the following:

Dry white wine, red wine, port, brandy, rum, sherry (a splash of dry sherry is often used in Chinese stir-fries), madeira, beer.

### The freezer

I have never been a great advocate of freezers it's a point of professional pride but I do use them to store food that has a very short season when fresh, such as corn, peas, and fava beans. I also find them convenient for storing some pasta, and puff and filo pastry.

It is well worth keeping a stock of ice cream vanilla and chocolate to prepare simple desserts and to serve as an accompaniment to hot or cold desserts.

# THOUGHTFUL SHOPPING WITH THE **SEASONS**

In a professional kitchen, chefs have access to good-quality raw materials on a daily basis from a varying list of suppliers. This means we provide our clientele with all their favorite foods throughout the year. To many people this may sound wonderful, but I find it somewhat sad, because I believe in the idea of seasonality in foods.

Nowadays, large supermarkets are also crammed full of exotic foods flown in from around the globe, thanks to advances in transportation and the higher expectations of shoppers.

Tomatoes, asparagus, and strawberries, for example, are now available throughout the year. Tomatoes have often been picked far too early, and therefore lack flavor because they are underripe. The ripening process continues on their transportation to the supermarkets, instead of on the vine. Taste the difference between these tomatoes and those picked in the height of the summer season. They not only taste better, but they are also less expensive because they are plentiful. The same can be said of strawberries, asparagus and many other ingredients.

A farmers' market or road-side stall is far more likely than a supermarket to reflect the seasons, with lower prices when there is a glut. In a nutshell, if you cook with the seasons in mind, you will eat better and spend less. Shop often and plan your menus accordingly.

# SPRING

For me, the best spring dishes are simple, reflecting the delicacy of the new season, but are nonetheless full of fresh tastes and bright colors.

The glowing reds and distinctive flavors of rhubarb and beets are shown at their best in simple dishes. So, too, are the many shades of green, characteristic of springtime, found in asparagus, fava beans, peas, and fresh young spinach. In England, May is the traditional month for asparagus, although the exact weeks will depend on the weather. The same is true of fava beans and peas. A few warm weeks will also see British-grown watercress.

New potatoes now seem to be available all year round, but purple-sprouting broccoli is a springtime speciality of British growers. Also look out for spring cabbage varieties and (unhearted) spring greens.

If you know a good source for fresh fish, now is the time to buy crab, wild salmon, and trout.

Spring cookery should exploit all the freshness of this abundant season, with minimum artifice.

# SUMMER

During the hottest months of the year, seasonal produce and cooking retains the light touch and fresh feel of spring (think of the variety of salad greens), but has the added punch of sun-ripened flavors and colors: Juicy red tomatoes, cherries, strawberries, blueberries, golden and purple plums. Gooseberries appear, as do raspberries. Peaches, nectarines, and melons are also at their prime.

The vegetables are crisp and succulent: Zucchini, broccoli, string and runner beans. Artichokes are available, and corn on the cob appears in late summer.

Salads are full of flavor, color, and texture, with cucumber, celery, tomatoes, and fresh raw beets.

Herrings, mackerel, and squid join crab on the summer menu.

With a palette of nature's colors, tastes, and textures before us, food shopping and cooking is an inexpensive and easy pleasure.

# FALL

The countryside seems to turn to gold as we reap the harvests of
our fields and orchards, taking advantage of the last warm days for
apple and blackberry picking. In the fall we get a choice of
traditional apple varieties: Don't miss them, as many appear in
supermarkets for a very short season. Pears and several types of
plum, including damsons, are also harvested now, as are walnuts
and hazelnuts. Luscious pomegranates and figs are fresh now too.

Mussels, clams, scallops, and oysters come back into season, and
cod and plenty of other white fish are tasty and easily available.

Late summer and early fall see the arrival of sun-ripened
eggplant and bell peppers; corn on the cob and zucchini continue to
be good. Now is also the time to go hunting for wild mushrooms
(never eat anything you are in the slightest doubt about). As fall
progresses, cauliflowers and leeks get better.

As the evenings draw in and the weather turns chilly, our
thoughts turn to warming bowls of soup, and what better ingredient
than fall's great golden-orange prize, the pumpkin. Other winter
squash come in all shapes and sizes, making fall food buying and
cooking just as adventurous as in summer.

# WINTER

This season's tasty and comforting root vegetables are perfect for rustling up casserole dishes and soups to keep out the cold. With so many different cooking methods–roasting, frying, stewing, mashing– they need never be boring. The variety is almost endless, and includes Jerusalem artichokes, parsnips, turnips, rutabaga, celeriac, scorzonera, and salsify (a long, thin root, sometimes called oyster plant).

The brassica family provides the bright colors of Savoy and red cabbages, little Brussels sprouts, and curly kale.

Apples and pears should still be available at good prices. Traditional foods for the Christmas season, some imported, include cranberries, chestnuts, brazil nuts, pineapples, lychees, and a wide variety of citrus fruits.

At the fish market, good cheap mussels are joined by bargain smelts and skate.

Cabbages and root vegetables are also the perfect partners to winter's other speciality, game; it's not always expensive, so be ready to take advantage of bargains.

# A FEW REMARKS ABOUT **MENU** PLANNING

When thinking about what foods go well together, I often base menus around certain cuisines or styles of cooking (for example, Italian, French, Greek, Thai, Chinese, or South American).

Once you understand the spirit of the dish or the style of cooking, feel free to improvise and make changes. Discovering new taste combinations is, for me, the most exciting and creative aspect of cooking.

Remember to plan your time sensibly. For most people, the first attempt at a dish may take twice as long as expected. Plan menus to include only one untried recipe or lengthy preparation, making the other courses a little easier.

Other aspects of menu planning may seem obvious, but it's worth taking a few minutes to make sure you have a variety of colors, flavors, and textures. Choose accompanying salads, vegetables, sauces, and garnishes to add contrast where needed.

Here are some menu suggestions using combinations of recipes featured in the book. Plan ahead, allow time to give them your best shot, and enjoy them!

# MENU SUGGESTIONS

## ORIGINAL SUNDAY TIMES MENU
$2 for 4
Spicy Mexican Barbecue Bean Soup
Hot Dog Fusilli
Cinnamon Baked Apples "en papillote"

## ITALIAN VERVE
$8 for 4
Verdura Tonnato
Turkey Osso Buco
Coffee Risotto

## SOUTH AMERICAN FEEL
$8 for 4
Ceviche of Whiting
Grilled Chicken Wings
on Drunken Black beans
with Chili Verde

## ENGLISH FARE
$8 for 4
B.L.T. Salad
Soft Roe Potato Cakes
with Caper Mayo
Apple Bread and Butter Sponge pudding

## GREEK FLAVORS
$2 for 4
Avgolemono
Lentil Moussaka Tart

## SUMMER PICNIC
$6 for 4
Arrancini
Verdura Tonnato
Caraway, Onion, and Bacon Tart

## MEDITERRANEAN INSPIRED
$8 for 4
Sambusak
(Cheese and Potato Cornish Pasties)
Cod Tagine

## HOT AND COLD PASTA BUFFET
$6 for 4
Jumbled Pasta, Chickpea, and
Basil Salad

Spaghetti with Potatoes and Wilted
Beans
Trenette with Tuna and Tomatoes

## DINNER IN AN HOUR OR LESS
$8 for 4
Pesto Baked Mushrooms
Grey Mullet in Acqua Pazza
Prune and Almond Frittata

## SUMMER EVENING BARBECUE
$8 for 4
Chargrilled Calamari Salad
Persian Koftas with Pita Toasts
Shanghai Fishburgers
Barbecue Spice Rub Chicken

# SOUPS

## Pumpkin bisque

Pumpkins are often underrated, but their mellow flavor makes them incredibly versatile, ideal for both sweet and savory dishes. It's certainly worth making the most of them when they appear in supermarkets in the fall.

Instead of bread and garlic in this recipe, you could use six to eight pieces of ready-made garlic bread.

1 oz butter
1 small onion, chopped
4 cups peeled pumpkin, seeds removed, cut into chunks
1½ cups milk
1½ cups chicken or vegetable broth
3 slices of white bread
2 garlic cloves, halved
salt and freshly ground pepper
freshly grated nutmeg

Heat the butter in a heavy-bottomed saucepan, add the onion and cook until soft and translucent. Add the pumpkin and cook, stirring occasionally, for 5 minutes longer. Add the milk and broth, and bring to a boil.

Meanwhile, lightly toast the bread, then rub with the cut cloves of garlic, and cut each slice into four pieces. Add to a boiling soup and reduce heat to a simmer. Cook for about 30 minutes or until the pumpkin is tender.

Pour into a blender and blend to a fine, creamy-textured purée. If the soup is too thick you may need to add a little more milk. Season to taste with salt, pepper, and nutmeg; serve hot.

## Mussel chowder

Chowders are normally associated with clams, but I find them tough and tasteless–give me mussels any day. If you are feeling extravagant, add a pinch of saffron to the chowder with the milk and cream; its flavor goes beautifully with mussels.

2 lb fresh mussels, scrubbed and debearded
½ oz butter
2 strips of bacon, cut into small pieces
1 onion, chopped
½ leek, cut into small cubes
1 carrot, cut into small cubes
1 garlic clove, crushed
2 cups potatoes, cut into small cubes
½ cup milk
5 tablespoons light cream
fresh parsley, chopped
salt and freshly ground pepper

Put the mussels in a large saucepan, add 1½ cups water, cover with a tight-fitting lid, and bring to a boil over high heat. Cook for 2 minutes or until the mussels open. Drain them in a colander, retaining the cooking liquid. Remove the mussels from their shells; discard the shells.

Heat the butter in a heavy-bottomed saucepan, add the bacon, onion, leek, carrot, and garlic, and cook for 2 minutes or until the vegetables are tender. Strain the mussel cooking liquid and add to the pan, then add the potatoes. Bring to a boil, then reduce heat and simmer until the potatoes are cooked.

Add the milk and cream, chopped parsley, and mussels. Season to taste with pepper and salt if required; serve hot.

## Avgolemono
## (Greek egg and lemon soup)

I discovered this soup while on vacation on the island of Corfu in Greece. I loved its simplicity and tanginess, and couldn't wait to try making it myself. Basmati rice, while not authentic, adds a lovely fragrance to the soup. I sometimes serve it lightly chilled.

3½ cups chicken broth
¼ cup long-grain rice (preferably basmati)
2 eggs
3 tablespoons fresh lemon juice
salt and freshly ground pepper

Bring the broth to a boil in a saucepan, add the rice, and simmer until the rice is cooked and tender, about 12 minutes.

Break the eggs into a bowl, add the lemon juice, and whisk until light and frothy.

A little at a time, stir the cooked rice and hot liquid into the eggs, until all is blended together. Return to the pan and cook over low heat, stirring all the time, until the soup thickens enough to coat the back of a spoon–it must not be allowed to boil. Season to taste with salt and pepper, and serve at once. Alternatively, let cool, then chill.

## Roasted corn broth
## with chunky pea guacamole

3 ears of corn
2 oz butter, melted
salt and freshly ground pepper
2½ cups chicken or vegetable broth
1½ cups cooked black beans
½ cups Cheddar cheese, coarsely shredded

**For the pea guacamole:**
1½ cups cooked peas
1 small green chili pepper, halved, deseeded, and finely chopped
2 tomatoes, deseeded and cut into small pieces
3 tablespoons fresh cilantro, chopped
3 tablespoons scallions, finely chopped
1 teaspoon fresh lime juice
pinch of ground cumin

Preheat the oven to 400°F.

Put the ears of corn on a baking sheet, brush with the butter, sprinkle with salt and pepper, and cook until tender and lightly browned; this will take 20–25 minutes. Turn the corn regularly so they brown evenly.

Remove from the oven and, when cool enough to handle, hold the corn over a chopping board and use a knife to scrape off all the kernels; reserve the kernels. Cut the cobs into chunks and return to the oven to roast for another 10 minutes.

Bring the broth to a boil in a saucepan, add the roasted cobs, reduce the heat and simmer for 40–45 minutes. Strain the corn broth through a strainer and season to taste.

To make the pea guacamole, mash the peas with a fork, add the remaining ingredients, and season to taste.

To serve, divide the guacamole between four soup plates or bowls, add the reserved corn kernels and the black beans, then pour over the broth and top with the shredded cheese; serve at once.

## Green tomato gazpacho

At the end of summer, gardeners often find they have a glut of green tomatoes. This chilled soup is a great way to use them up and, of course, it is just as good with red tomatoes. I like to serve gazpacho topped with a spoonful of sour cream mixed with a little chopped fresh basil.

2 slices of white bread, crusts removed
1 lb green tomatoes, roughly chopped
1 green bell pepper, halved, deseeded, and roughly chopped
½ cucumber, cut into chunks
½ onion, roughly chopped
1 garlic clove, crushed
½ teaspoon coriander seeds, crushed
6 tablespoons olive oil
5 tablespoons white wine vinegar
salt and freshly ground pepper
sugar

Put the bread in a small bowl and pour about 2cups of cold water over it.

Put the tomatoes, pepper, cucumber, onion, garlic, and coriander seeds in a blender and blend to a smooth purée. Strain the purée through a fine strainer into a bowl.

Squeeze the water from the bread and put the bread in the blender. Blend to a pulp, then, with the machine running, add the olive oil a little at a time until incorporated into the bread. Add the vinegar, a good pinch of salt, and 5 tablespoons of the strained tomato mixture. Blend for another 30 seconds.

Stir the bread mixture into the bowl of tomato mixture. Adjust the consistency by adding a little more water if necessary. Season to taste, adding a pinch of sugar and more vinegar if required. Chill the gazpacho until ready to serve.

## Frozen fava bean and lemongrass vichyssoise

This variation on the classic, creamy, chilled vichyssoise has a subtle and delicate flavor; it is just as delicious made with peas instead of fava beans.

3 oz butter
½ cup leeks, roughly chopped
2 stalks of lemongrass, chopped
½ teaspoon fresh root ginger, chopped
3½ cups chicken or vegetable broth
6 cups frozen fava beans, shelled
1 cup milk
salt and freshly ground pepper
sugar
4 sprigs of mint, finely chopped

Heat the butter in a saucepan, add the leeks, lemongrass, and ginger, and cook over low heat until soft. Add the broth, bring to a boil, and simmer for 10 minutes. Add the shelled beans, return to a boil, then remove from the heat.

Pour into a blender and blend to a purée. (For a really smooth soup, strain through a strainer.) Add the milk and season to taste with salt, pepper, and a pinch of sugar. Chill until ready to serve. Sprinkle with chopped mint just before serving.

## Cabbage, turnip, and blood sausage soup

1 Savoy cabbage
2 large turnips
5 tablespoons olive oil
1 garlic clove, crushed
3½ cups chicken broth
¼ lb blood sausage (black pudding), thinly sliced
salt and freshly ground black pepper

Remove and discard the outside leaves of the cabbage, then cut the cabbage into about 1 inch pieces. Peel the turnips and cut them in half, then into ¼ inch thick slices.

Heat half the oil in a large saucepan, add the garlic and cabbage, and cook until the cabbage starts to soften. Add the sliced turnips, season lightly, and cook for 2–3 minutes longer. Pour in the broth, bring to a boil, reduce the heat, and simmer for 20–25 minutes or until the turnips are tender.

Add the blood sausage, season to taste, and simmer gently for a 2 minutes longer. Serve hot, in bowls, drizzled with the remaining olive oil, and sprinkled with some coarsely ground black pepper, accompanied by crusty French bread.

## French onion soup with herring crostini

**A classic warming soup with a fishy twist!**

3 tablespoons olive oil
2 oz butter
1 lb onions, thinly sliced
2 teaspoons sugar
1 small garlic clove, crushed
1 tablespoon tomato paste
½ cup white wine
3½ cups chicken broth

**For the herring crostini:**
8 oz can of herrings in oil
salt and freshly ground pepper
¾ cup Cheddar or Gruyère cheese, grated
1 small French bread

Heat the oil and butter in a large saucepan, add the onions, and sauté until tender. Sprinkle with the sugar and continue to cook until the sugar caramelizes and the onions turn a beautiful dark brown.

Add the garlic and tomato paste and cook, stirring once or twice, for another 5 minutes. Pour in the wine and broth, bring to a boil, reduce the heat, and simmer for 30–35 minutes.

To make the herring crostini, mash the herrings in a bowl, and season lightly. Cut the french bread into eight ½ inch slices, toast them, and spread with the mashed herring. Keep warm. Preheat the broiler to its highest setting.

Pour the hot soup into heatproof bowls, top each with two herring crostini, and sprinkle with cheese. Put the bowls under the hot broiler until the cheese is brown and bubbling. Serve at once.

## Tourin blanchi
## (Garlic soup)

This delicious, rich, garlic soup has only one drawback–its lingering flavor. It is probably best kept for close friends and consenting adults!

1 tablespoon olive oil
1 large onion, thinly sliced
1 whole head of garlic, cut into cloves, peeled and thinly sliced
¼ cup flour
2½ cups chicken broth
2 eggs
1 teaspoon white wine vinegar
salt and freshly ground pepper

Heat the oil in a heavy-bottomed saucepan, add the onion and garlic, and cook over low heat until soft. Stir in the flour and continue to cook over low heat, stirring frequently, for 1 minute to allow the flour to cook.

Add the broth a little at a time, stirring well until all is incorporated. Bring to a boil, reduce heat, and simmer gently for 30 minutes.

Pour into a blender and blend to a smooth purée.

Separate the eggs, beat the yolks with the vinegar, and whisk the whites lightly.

When ready to serve, return the puréed soup to a boil, then remove from heat. Gradually beat in the egg whites, then the yolks, season to taste, and serve at once (do not allow the soup to boil after the eggs have been added).

## Spicy Mexican barbecue bean soup

A last-minute garnish of chopped crisp bacon goes well with this soup.

3 tablespoons olive oil
1 onion, chopped
¼ teaspoon red pepper flakes
1 potato, cut into small pieces
14 oz canned baked beans in tomato sauce
1 cup chicken or vegetable broth
1 tablespoon brown sugar
1 teaspoon mustard
1 tablespoon molasses (optional)
salt and freshly ground pepper

Heat the oil in a saucepan, add the onion, and cook until soft. Add the red pepper flakes and cook for about 1 minute to release the flavor, then add the potato and most of the beans (reserve 5 tablespoons for garnishing the soup). Stir well, add the broth, and cook over low heat for 15–20 minutes or until the potato is nearly tender.

Combine the sugar, mustard, molasses, salt, and pepper. Add to the soup and cook for 5 minutes longer.

Pour into a blender and blend to a smooth purée. Taste and adjust the seasoning if required. Serve hot, garnished with the reserved beans.

## Dal soup with toasted cumin and rocket oil

Lentils and cumin are a marriage made in heaven, their earthy, nutty flavors complementing each other perfectly. The rocket adds a peppery touch.

1 litre (1¾ pints) chicken or vegetable broth
1 teaspoon cumin seeds, toasted and ground
½ teaspoon ground coriander
⅛ teaspoon cayenne pepper
1 small bay leaf
225 g (8 oz) lentils, rinsed
2 tablespoons olive oil
1 carrot, chopped
½ onion, chopped
salt and freshly ground pepper

### For the rocket oil:
1 tablespoon fresh lemon juice
3 tablespoons olive oil
50 g (2 oz) rocket

Bring the broth to a boil in a saucepan, add the toasted cumin, coriander, cayenne and bay leaf. Add the lentils, reduce the heat and simmer until tender, about 50 minutes.

Heat the oil in a small saucepan, add the carrot and onion and cook over low heat until soft.

Add this mixture to the simmering lentils and cook for a further 10–15 minutes.

To make the rocket oil, place the lemon juice, olive oil and rocket in a blender together with a little salt and pepper and blend just long enough to form a coarse purée.

Remove the bay leaf from the soup, then pour into a blender and blend to a coarse purée. Divide the soup between four soup plates or bowls, top each with a spoonful of the rocket oil and serve hot. Toasted croûtons are a good addition.

## Thai chicken broth

750 ml (1¼ pints) chicken broth
16 marinated Thai chicken wings (page 38)
200 g (7 oz) canned tomatoes, drained and chopped
½ teaspoon shredded fresh root ginger
100 g (4 oz) button mushrooms, sliced
50 g (2 oz) Chinese cabbage, shredded
4 scallions, finely chopped
2 tablespoons light soy sauce
pinch of red pepper flakes
2 tablespoons fresh cilantro leaves

Put the broth in a large saucepan and bring to a simmer. Add the chicken wings, tomatoes and ginger and poach very gently for 15–20 minutes or until the wings are cooked. Remove the wings and keep warm.

Skim off any impurities that have risen to the surface of the broth, add the mushrooms, cabbage and scallions and simmer for 2 minutes.

Stir in the soy sauce, chili flakes and cilantro, taste and adjust the seasoning if required. Divide the chicken wings between four soup plates or bowls, ladle on the soup and serve hot.

# APPETIZERS AND SALADS

## Pesto baked mushrooms

This stuffing can also be used for tomatoes, zucchini, eggplant, or onions, although they will take longer to cook (15–20 minutes for zucchini and 45–55 minutes for eggplant and onions).

4 cups large button mushrooms
4 tablespoons olive oil
1 onion, chopped
2 zucchini, chopped
1 small jar of pesto sauce, about ½ cup
¼-½ cup Parmesan cheese, shredded
1 egg yolk
salt and freshly ground pepper

Gently pull out the stalks from the mushrooms and chop the stalks finely. Heat half the oil in a skillet, add the chopped onion, zucchini, and mushroom stalks, and cook over low heat until soft, about 5 minutes. Let mixture become cold.

Preheat the oven to 400°F.

Place the onion mixture in a blender with the pesto sauce and blend to a coarse paste. Add enough Parmesan to form a thicker paste. Transfer to a bowl and stir in the egg yolk. Taste and adjust the seasoning.

Lightly sauté the mushroom caps in the remaining oil for 1 minute, then drain. Fill each cap with the pesto stuffing, place on a baking sheet, and bake for 5–8 minutes or until tender when tested with a small sharp knife. Alternatively, cook the mushrooms under a hot broiler. Serve hot.

## Oriental mushroom fritters with peanut curry dip

vegetable oil for deep-fat frying
4 cups button mushrooms
3 tablespoons five-spice powder
½ teaspoon red pepper flakes
1¼ cups cornstarch
½ teaspoon baking powder
salt and freshly ground black pepper
1 egg white

### For the peanut curry dip:
½ cup chicken or vegetable broth
½ teaspoon curry powder
½ garlic clove, crushed
½ teaspoon honey
3 tablespoons peanut butter
½ teaspoon light soy sauce
dash of wine vinegar

Heat 3 tablespoons of oil in a skillet and sauté the mushrooms for 2 minutes or until they begin to soften. Season with five-spice powder and red pepper flakes, transfer to a bowl, and let mushrooms become cold.

To make the peanut curry dip, place all the ingredients in a saucepan and bring to a boil; simmer gently for 3–4 minutes, then let cool.

Put the cornstarch and baking powder in a bowl with ½ cup iced water, 4 tablespoons oil, and a little salt and pepper, and mix until smooth. When you are ready to sauté the mushrooms, whisk the egg white until stiff, then fold into the batter.

Heat the oil for deep-fat frying to 350°F (until a cube of bread browns in 30 seconds). Dip the mushrooms in the batter, then into the hot oil, and sauté until golden, 1–2 minutes. Drain well and serve with the peanut dip.

## Mexican dirty rice salad

A substantial salad that can be equally well served as a vegetarian main course, especially with plenty of Mexican garnishes; chopped avocado and tomato, sour cream and coarsely shredded Cheddar cheese.

2 oz butter
1 cup long-grain rice
1 green chili pepper, deseeded and chopped
1 teaspoon ground cumin
2 cups vegetable broth
salt and freshly ground pepper
1¾ cups canned black beans
4 scallions, finely chopped
3 tablespoons fresh cilantro, chopped

**For the dressing:**
6 tablespoons vegetable oil
1½ tablespoons white wine vinegar
1 teaspoon mustard

Heat the butter in a wide saucepan over low heat, add the rice, and cook, stirring, until opaque. Add the chili pepper and cumin, stir well, and cook for 1 minute longer.

Bring the broth to a boil, add to the rice with 1 teaspoon salt, and bring back to a boil. Reduce heat, cover with a tight-fitting lid, and cook for 20 minutes or until the rice is tender.

Drain the rice and transfer to a large bowl. Add the black beans, chopped scallions and cilantro, and mix well. Let cool slightly.

Put the dressing ingredients in a bowl and whisk together, then pour over the rice salad and serve at room temperature.

## Crispy Malaysian vegetable salad

½ cup broccoli, cut into small flowerets
2 carrots, cut into matchsticks
½ red bell pepper, deseeded and cut into matchsticks
½ yellow bell pepper, deseeded and cut into matchsticks
½ cucumber, cut into matchsticks
1 cup beansprouts
4 scallions, finely chopped
½ bunch of watercress
3 tablespoons roasted peanuts

**For the dressing:**
4 tablespoons lime juice
1 tablespoon fresh mint, chopped
1 tablespoon fresh cilantro, chopped
pinch of red pepper flakes
3 tablespoons light soy sauce
3 tablespoons sugar
½ cup vegetable oil

Put all the dressing ingredients in a bowl and whisk together. This can be made up to 2 days ahead and kept in the refrigerator.

Blanch the broccoli in boiling salted water until just tender but retaining a little crunchiness. Rinse under cold water, drain, and dry on paper towels.

Place all the vegetables in a bowl, add the watercress and the dressing, mix well, and leave for up to 15 minutes before serving, sprinkled with the roasted peanuts.

## Baked tomatoes with coddled eggs

4 large beefsteak tomatoes
salt and freshly ground pepper
4 eggs
1½ oz butter

Preheat the oven to 325°F.

Slice the tops off the tomatoes and scoop out the cores, seeds, and juice. Sprinkle a little salt and pepper inside the tomato shells, then put them in a lightly buttered oven-safe dish.

Break each egg into a cup, then slide into the tomato shells. Put a little knob of butter on each egg and season with a little more salt and pepper.

Bake the tomatoes for 12–15 minutes or until the egg whites are firm but the yolks are still soft.

Serve hot, topped with a spoonful of tapenade, pesto, or chili verde (page 74).

## Thai chicken wings in spiced coconut milk

1 teaspoon curry paste
1 small garlic clove, crushed
¼ teaspoon red pepper flakes
½ teaspoon ground coriander
½ teaspoon turmeric
salt and freshly ground pepper
sugar
1 cup coconut milk
4 tablespoons vegetable oil
20 fresh chicken wings, boned

Put the curry paste, garlic, red pepper flakes, spices, salt, pepper, and a pinch of sugar in a bowl, add the coconut milk and oil, and whisk together. Add the chicken wings and turn to coat them in the marinade. Cover and put in the refrigerator for up to 24 hours.

To serve, soak four or more bamboo skewers in cold water for 30 minutes. Preheat the broiler or barbecue. Remove the chicken wings from the marinade and thread them onto the soaked skewers. Broil or barbecue until cooked and golden, turning occasionally; about 5–8 minutes.

I like to serve them with basmati rice, a crisp salad, and a dip made from ½ cup mayonnaise mixed with 3 tablespoons chopped mango chutney. They are also very good on their own, as cocktail nibbles, or you can use them in the Thai chicken broth (page 33).

## Salad of sardines "Monégasque"

The name comes from a Provençal word for Monaco, and this salad is full of the distinctive ingredients of the south of France; whenever I prepare it I dream of traveling through Provence, stopping for a light lunch and a glass of wine.

1½ cups new potatoes
1½ cups dried penne pasta
2 tomatoes, cut into quarters
2 hard-boiled eggs, shelled
½ small onion, cut into rings
4 red radishes
1 teaspoon capers, drained
1 cup canned sardines

### For the dressing:
2 teaspoons white wine vinegar
6 teaspoons olive oil
½ teaspoon anchovy extract
½ garlic clove, crushed
salt and freshly ground pepper

Boil the potatoes in salted water. At the same time, cook the pasta in plenty of boiling salted water, to which a little oil has been added to prevent the pasta from sticking together.

When the potatoes are tender, drain, peel, and slice them into a bowl. When the pasta is cooked al dente (just tender, but still firm to the bite), drain in a colander and add to the potatoes. Add the tomatoes, eggs, onion rings, radishes, and capers, and toss gently.

Drain the sardines, reserving the oil. Put the dressing ingredients in a bowl and whisk together with the sardine oil. Season to taste, then add to the salad, and toss gently to mix.

Serve the salad on a serving platter, topped with the sardines. I like to garnish this dish with crunchy deep-fat fried parsley.

## B.L.T. salad
## (Bacon, liver, and tomato salad)

My version of the infamous B.L.T. (normally a sandwich made with bacon, lettuce, and tomatoes). My ingredients are bacon, chicken livers, and tomatoes, transformed into a delicious warm salad.

½ cup olive oil
¾ lb fresh chicken livers, cleaned and halved
½ teaspoon ground cumin
6 tomatoes, halved
4 strips of bacon
3 tablespoons fresh cilantro leaves, roughly chopped
½ cup balsamic vinegar
mixed salad greens

Heat half the oil in a skillet until very hot, add the chicken livers, seasoned with a little cumin, and cook for 2–3 minutes, stirring occasionally, until brown and crisp on the outside, yet still pink and tender inside.

Preheat the broiler. Brush the tomatoes with a little olive oil. Broil the bacon and tomatoes until the bacon is crisp and the tomatoes are soft but not mushy. Sprinkle the tomatoes with some of the cilantro, and keep the bacon and tomatoes warm.

Remove the livers from the skillet and keep warm. Add the vinegar to the pan and bring to a boil. Whisk in the remaining olive oil.

Toss the salad greens with some of the warm dressing and arrange on four plates. Crumble the crispy bacon over the greens and put three tomato halves on each plate. Top with the chicken livers and drizzle the remaining dressing over the livers. Garnish with the remaining cilantro leaves.

## Caraway, onion, and bacon tart

3 tablespoons butter
4 strips of bacon, chopped
4 onions, thinly sliced
2 teaspoons caraway seeds
salt and freshly ground pepper
2 eggs
2 egg yolks
1 cup double cream

### For the pastry:
2½ cups all-purpose flour
pinch of salt
5 oz butter or margarine

To make the pastry, sift the flour and salt into a bowl, and rub in the butter or margarine until the mixture resembles fine breadcrumbs. Add just enough water to bind, then let rest in the refrigerator for 30 minutes before using.

Preheat the oven to 400°F.

Roll out the pastry and use to line a 9 inch buttered pie pan. Prick the base evenly with a fork, line it with wax paper, fill it with baking beans, and bake blind for 6–8 minutes. Remove the paper and beans and return the pastry case to the oven for 5 minutes or until cooked and lightly golden, then let cool.

Heat the butter in a skillet, add the chopped bacon, and cook until crisp. Remove the bacon, add the onions and caraway seeds to the pan with a little salt and pepper, and cook over low heat until golden and tender, then let cool slightly.

Arrange the onions and bacon in the pastry case. Beat the eggs and yolks with the cream and a little salt and pepper, pour over the onions and bacon, and bake for 30 minutes or until golden and set. Serve warm.

## White bean hummus with yogurt

**An alternative to the usual hummus made with chickpeas.**

1⅓ cups canned cannellini beans
2 garlic cloves, crushed
3 tablespoons tahini (sesame seed paste)
juice of 1 lemon
½ teaspoon ground cumin
4 tablespoons olive oil
3 tablespoons plain yogurt
salt
1 tablespoon fresh parsley, chopped

Drain the cannellini beans and put them in a blender or food processor with the remaining ingredients, except the parsley. Blend to a smooth paste. Taste and add more salt, garlic, or lemon juice if required. Refrigerate overnight.

To serve, sprinkle with the parsley, and drizzle with a little olive oil. I sometimes add a garnish of chopped black olives and cubed tomatoes as well.

## Jumbled pasta, chickpea, and basil salad

This salad is a great way to use up those odd packages of pasta that are never quite enough to make a whole dish on their own. For a real treat, top the pasta salad with some freshly shredded pecorino cheese.

½ cup dried chickpeas or 1 cup canned chickpeas
½ lb mixed dried pasta
2 ripe tomatoes, deseeded and chopped
½ cup fresh or frozen fava beans, cooked
½ onion, thinly sliced
4 tablespoons fresh basil or parsley, chopped

**For the dressing:**
5 tablespoons olive oil
½ garlic clove, crushed
1 tablespoon red wine vinegar
¼ teaspoon red pepper flakes
salt and freshly ground pepper

If using dried chickpeas, soak them overnight in plenty of cold water. The next day, drain them well, put in a saucepan, cover with fresh cold water, and bring to a boil (do not add salt or the chickpeas will harden and be difficult to cook). Reduce heat and simmer for about 1½ hours or until tender. When cooked, drain well, and put in a bowl.

Cook the pasta in boiling salted water to which a little oil has been added to prevent the pasta from sticking together. When the pasta is cooked al dente (just tender, but still firm to the bite), drain well and add to the chickpeas.

While the pasta and chickpeas are still warm, put all the dressing ingredients in a bowl and whisk together. Pour over the pasta and chickpeas and let cool.

Just before serving, add the chopped tomatoes, fava beans, onion, and herbs. For the best results serve at room temperature, not chilled.

## Verdura tonnato

Here the classic tonnato sauce, which usually accompanies cold poached veal, is served as a dip for a selection of crisp raw vegetables.

8 oz can of tuna, drained
1 teaspoon anchovy extract
1 teaspoon capers, drained
3 tablespoons fresh lemon juice
salt and freshly ground pepper
½ cup mayonnaise

Put the tuna, anchovy extract and capers in a blender and blend to a smooth paste. Add the lemon juice, salt and pepper, and transfer to a bowl. Add the mayonnaise and beat with the tuna mixture. Add a little water if it is too thick. Serve with vegetable crudités (carrots, green beans, cucumber, celeriac).

## Asian spiced herrings with fruit raita

1 teaspoon red pepper flakes
½ garlic clove, crushed
1 teaspoon ground ginger
1 teaspoon garam masala
salt and freshly ground black pepper
½ cup vegetable or olive oil
1 lb fresh herrings, cleaned and cut into 2 inch pieces

### For the raita sauce:
½ cup plain yogurt
½ teaspoon ground cumin
2 teaspoons fresh cilantro or mint, chopped
1 firm banana

In a shallow dish, mix together the red pepper flakes, garlic, ginger, garam masala, salt, and pepper. Add 3 tablespoons of the oil and mix to a paste. Add the fish pieces and let marinate for 30 minutes.

To make the raita, mix together the yogurt, cumin, and cilantro or mint in a bowl. Coarsely shred the banana into the yogurt, stir gently to mix, and season to taste.

Heat the remaining 5 tablespoons oil in a skillet and sauté the herring pieces until golden, about 4 minutes on each side. Drain on paper towels and serve hot, accompanied by the raita.

## Ceviche of whiting

In some parts of South America oranges are used instead of limes.

1 lb very fresh fillet of whiting
juice of 2 limes
salt
1 tablespoon coriander seeds, crushed
5 tablespoons olive oil
½ tablespoon ketchup
dash of Tobasco sauce
1 small onion, finely sliced
2 tomatoes, skinned, deseeded and cut into small dice
½ cup cucumber, peeled and cut into small cubes
1 tablespoon fresh cilantro, chopped, plus extra to garnish
corn tortillas, fried until crisp

Cut the fish into ¾ inch cubes and put in a bowl. Pour on the lime juice and a little salt and toss well to coat the fish. Cover the bowl and put it in the refrigerator for up to 5 hours, stirring from time to time. The fish will become opaque.

Drain off the juice and combine some of it (according to taste—you may not need all of it) with the crushed coriander seeds, oil, ketchup, and Tobasco to form a dressing. Pour the dressing over the fish and gently stir in the onion, tomatoes, cucumber, and fresh cilantro. Refrigerate for 1 hour more.

Serve chilled, layered between the tortilla crisps. Garnish with fresh cilantro.

## Arrancini

Arrancini is the Italian term for small oranges; these look-alikes are made of red salmon bound with cooked rice and fried until crisp. The traditional accompaniment is a well-flavored tomato sauce. Tartare sauce or a pesto-flavored mayonnaise are also good.

1cup arborio rice
1 hard-boiled egg, chopped
8 oz can of red salmon, drained and flaked
1 teaspoon fresh parsley, chopped
½ teaspoon dried or fresh oregano
salt and freshly ground pepper
1 egg, beaten
2½ cups fresh white breadcrumbs
vegetable oil for deep-fat frying
lemon wedges, to serve

Cook the rice in plenty of salted boiling water for 12–15 minutes or until just tender. Drain well and let dry for at least 30 minutes. (The rice can be cooked up to a day ahead and kept in the refrigerator.)

Put the cooked rice in a bowl, add the chopped hard-boiled egg, the flaked salmon, herbs, salt, and pepper. Refrigerate for 1 hour.

Shape the chilled mixture into tiny balls, about 1½ inches in diameter. Put the beaten egg in a saucer and the breadcrumbs on a plate. Roll the rice balls first in the beaten egg, then in the breadcrumbs.

Heat the oil for deep-fat frying to 350°F (until a cube of bread browns in 30 seconds). Sauté the rice balls for 3–4 minutes or until golden. Drain on paper towels and serve with lemon wedges.

## Tatin of sardines

2 cups (or 1 lb) puff pastry
1 oz butter
2 onions, thinly sliced
3 anchovy fillets, finely chopped
1¼ lb fresh sardines, filleted, central bones removed
salt and freshly ground pepper
⅓ cup olive oil
½ garlic clove, crushed
½ teaspoon coriander seeds, crushed
3 tomatoes, deseeded and cubed
juice of ½ lemon

Preheat the oven to 400°F.

Roll out the pastry on a lightly floured board to approximately ¼ inch thick. Using a 4 inch round cutter, cut out four pastry circles, prick each thoroughly with a fork and bake for 8–10 minutes or until cooked and golden. Remove from the oven and let cool.

Meanwhile, heat the butter in a saucepan, add the sliced onions, and cook gently until golden, then add the chopped anchovies. Spread each baked tart with the onion and anchovy mixture. Arrange the sardine fillets on top. Season and brush with a little of the olive oil. Put in a hot oven for 5–6 minutes or until the sardines are cooked and lightly browned.

While the tarts are cooking, prepare a light sauce: Heat the remaining oil in a saucepan, add the garlic and coriander seeds, and heat gently. Add the cubed tomatoes, lemon juice, and salt and pepper, and warm through to soften the tomatoes. Pour the sauce around the tarts and serve hot.

## Charbroiled calamari salad

However you cook them, squid need a very short cooking time, otherwise they will toughen. If you want to cook them on a barbecue, leave them whole and cut them into rings when cooked. If you prefer your squid to be crispy, dip the rings in breadcrumbs, and deep-fat fry until golden. There are several good brands of frozen squid (calamari) at very reasonable prices.

4 tomatoes, cut into quarters
6 black olives, pitted and halved
1 red onion, halved and thinly sliced
1 tablespoon fresh oregano leaves
1¼ lb squid, cleaned and cut into ¼ inch rings
salt and freshly ground pepper
2 Little Gem lettuces, or other crisp lettuce leaves

### For the sauce:
2 garlic cloves, crushed
⅓ cup olive oil
⅓ cup vegetable oil
1 egg
1 tablespoon white wine vinegar
dash of Worcestershire sauce
dash of Tobasco sauce

To make the sauce, whisk all the ingredients together in a bowl or blend in a blender.

Toss the tomatoes, olives, onion, and oregano together with just enough of the sauce to coat lightly.

Sprinkle the squid with a little salt and pepper, and broil for 1 minute under a hot broiler or in a cast-iron broiler pan.

Arrange the lettuce leaves on four plates, top with the tomato salad, then the broiled squid; serve warm.

## Beet "gravad mackerel"

Mackerel makes an interesting variation on the classic Scandinavian gravadlax (marinated salmon). Beets have a sweet taste that go well with the sweet dill and mustard sauce.

3 tablespoons sugar
4 tablespoons salt
a little freshly ground pepper
4 large, very fresh mackerel, cleaned and filleted
6 tablespoons fresh dill, chopped, plus extra to garnish
1 cooked fresh beet (not in vinegar), coarsely shredded
1 tablespoon capers (optional), to garnish
lemon wedges, to serve

### For the sauce:
3 tablespoons mustard
2 teaspoons brown sugar
1 tablespoon white wine vinegar
⅓ cup olive oil
3 tablespoons fresh dill, chopped

Mix the sugar, salt, and pepper together in a bowl. Lay the mackerel fillets out flat, skin side down, and sprinkle with the sugar and salt mixture. Cover each fillet with some of the chopped dill. Arrange the fillets head to tail in a shallow dish, just large enough to hold the fish. Sprinkle with the remaining dill, then cover with clingfilm and press down with a weighted board, about 2–3 lb. Refrigerate for 8 hours.

Sprinkle the shredded beet over the fish and return to the refrigerator for another 8 hours.

To make the sauce, mix the mustard, sugar and vinegar together in a bowl, whisk in the oil, add the dill, and season to taste.

To serve, scrape the dill mixture and beet from the fish and, using a long, sharp knife, cut the fillets into thin slices, beginning at the tail end.

Garnish with fresh dill and capers, if using. Serve with lemon wedges and serve the sauce separately.

## Soft roe potato cakes with caper mayo

½ lb soft herring roe (milt), cleaned
⅓ cup milk
1½ oz butter, softened
1 onion, finely chopped
1 cup cooked mashed potatoes
1 teaspoon fresh parsley, chopped
salt and freshly ground pepper
freshly grated nutmeg
2 large potatoes
4–5 tablespoons all-purpose flour
2 eggs, beaten
vegetable oil for cooking

### For the caper mayo:
½ cup mayonnaise
1 tablespoon capers, chopped
juice and shredded zest of 1 lemon

Poach the roe in the milk for 6–8 minutes, then drain, discarding the milk, and let cool.

Heat half the butter in a skillet, add the onion and cook until golden. Put the mashed potatoes in a bowl, add the onion and beat in the remaining butter until smooth. Cube the cooked roe and gently stir into the potatoes, together with the parsley. Season to taste with salt, pepper, and nutmeg. Refrigerate for 1 hour.

Mix the ingredients for the caper mayonnaise in a small bowl.

Peel and shred the potatoes, and dry them in a clean dish cloth. Divide the mashed potato mixture into eight pieces, then shape into ovals. Dip the potato cakes into the flour to coat lightly, then coat them with the beaten eggs, then finally coat them evenly with the shredded potatoes.

Heat the oil in a skillet and cook the potato cakes until golden and crisp on both sides, about 3–4 minutes. Drain on paper towels and serve hot, with the caper mayonnaise.

## Roe on toast

Soft roe, or milt, for me, is one of the greatest treasures at a budget price, but unfortunately it is seldom used. Try it simply on toast, for breakfast or brunch, and you will discover just what you have been missing. Malt vinegar is the traditional dressing.

2 oz butter
¾ lb soft herring roe (milt), cleaned
salt and freshly ground black pepper
4 slices of white bread
3 tablespoons malt vinegar

Heat the butter in a skillet, season the roe with salt and pepper, and sauté them until it begins to curl up and turn golden, about 1–2 minutes.

Meanwhile, toast the bread.

Arrange the roe on the toast and serve at once, sprinkled with the vinegar and a generous amount of black pepper.

## Thai mussels

Mussels are often served as a first course in restaurants, but because they are quite fiddly to eat, they are very filling, and can easily become the main event.

2 lb fresh mussels, scrubbed and debearded
3 tablespoons vegetable oil
½ onion, finely chopped
2 fresh red chili peppers, deseeded and finely chopped
(or ½ teaspoon red pepper flakes)
2 small garlic cloves, crushed
½ tablespoon brown sugar
1 tablespoon light soy sauce
3 tablespoons fresh mint, roughly chopped
freshly ground black pepper

Put the mussels in a skillet or a fairly shallow saucepan. Pour over ½ cup water, cover with a tight-fitting lid, and put over high heat until the shells open, about 2–3 minutes. Transfer the mussels to a serving dish.

Heat the oil in the cleaned skillet, add the onion, chili peppers, garlic, sugar, and soy sauce, and cook until tender. Pour the mixture over the mussels, sprinkle with the chopped mint and pepper, and serve at once.

## Broiled stuffed mussels with pico de gallo

Pico de gallo means "chicken's beak" in Spanish, and is the name given to a piquant salsa. You could add more Tobasco sauce to heighten the flavor, but take carenot to overwhelm the mussels.

2 lb fresh mussels, scrubbed and debearded
6 tablespoons white wine
½ cup fresh white breadcrumbs
salt and freshly ground pepper

**For the pico de gallo:**
8 oz can of tomatoes, drained and finely chopped
½ onion
½ garlic clove, crushed
½ teaspoon coriander seeds, crushed
1 tablespoon fresh cilantro
3 tablespoons lime juice
1 tablespoon maple syrup
6 tablespoons olive oil
2 drops of Tobasco sauce

Put the mussels in a skillet or a fairly shallow saucepan. Add the white wine and ½ cup of water, cover with a tight-fitting lid and put over a high heat until the shells open, about 2–3 minutes. Drain the mussels in a colander, strain the cooking liquid, and set aside.

Remove the mussels from their shells and discard the shells that have the inner muscle attached. Arrange the mussels in their half shells on a baking sheet.

Make the pico de gallo by placing all the ingredients in a blender or food processor and blending together. Pour the mixture into a bowl, add the breadcrumbs, and season lightly.

Put a little of the pico de gallo stuffing on each mussel half and cook under a preheated hot broiler until golden and crisp.

Put a little of the reserved mussel cooking liquid in the bottom of each serving bowl and top with the broiled mussels; serve at once.

# PASTA AND Co.

## Penne with caramelized celery, walnut, and sage gremolata

This is a delicious dish for vegetarians, but it is also very good with the addition of 2 strips of sautéed bacon.

3 oz butter
2½ cups celery, thinly sliced
1 teaspoon sugar
5 tablespoons red wine
1 tablespoon balsamic vinegar
3 tablespoons olive oil
1 lb penne pasta
salt and freshly ground pepper
freshly grated nutmeg

### For the gremolata:
½ cups walnuts
1½ cups fresh white breadcrumbs
½ garlic clove, crushed
1 tablespoon fresh sage, chopped

Heat 1 oz of the butter in a skillet, add the celery and sugar, and cook until soft and lightly golden. Pour in the wine and vinegar, and continue cooking to form a lightly caramelized glaze around the celery.

Put all the ingredients for the gremolata in a blender and blend together.

Heat the remaining butter in a skillet with the olive oil, add the gremolata, and cook until golden and crunchy.

Cook the pasta in boiling salted water until al dente (just tender, but still firm to the bite). Drain, and mix with the caramelized celery. Taste and adjust the seasoning, and serve hot, sprinkled with the gremolata.

## Fettucine with charred tomatoes and rosemary oil

If you know someone who owns a rosemary bush, you have a supply of fresh rosemary all year round. This hardy herb is not just for use with lamb. Here it makes a tasty oil for a simple pasta dish.

450 g (1 lb) small plum tomatoes, halved
1 garlic clove, crushed
1 tablespoon sugar
salt and freshly ground pepper
450 g (1 lb) fettucine pasta
6 tablespoons olive oil
40 g (1½ oz) fresh rosemary
freshly grated nutmeg

Preheat the oven to 400°F.

Put the tomatoe halves on a lightly greased baking sheet, rub each with half of the garlic, then sprinkle with sugar, and a little salt and pepper. Bake the tomatoes for 10–15 minutes or until soft and slightly charred. Alternatively, put them under a hot broiler to achieve the same result.

Cook the fettuccine in boiling salted water until al dente (just tender, but still firm to the bite), then drain.

Put the olive oil, rosemary, and remaining garlic in a blender and blend to a purée. Season to taste. Toss the pasta with the rosemary oil and adjust the seasoning with salt, pepper, and nutmeg. Top with the charred tomatoes and serve at once.

## Rigatoni with white bean hummus

1 lb rigatoni pasta
½ cup olive oil
5 tablespoons fresh parsley, chopped
½ cup White Bean Hummus (page 42)
salt and freshly ground black pepper

Cook the pasta in boiling salted water until al dente (just tender, but still firm to the bite). Drain the pasta, retaining a little of the cooking water.

Return the pasta to the pan, add the olive oil and parsley, then carefully stir in the White Bean Hummus and a little of the cooking water to form a sauce around the pasta. Season with salt and a good sprinkling of freshly ground black pepper, and serve hot.

## Parsley mash gnocchi with blue cheese

2 lb potatoes, peeled
salt and freshly ground pepper
2½ cups all-purpose flour
1 egg
freshly grated nutmeg
½ cup fresh parsley, chopped

### For the blue cheese sauce:
5 oz cold butter, cut into small pieces
1 cup blue cheese (e.g., Stilton), crumbled

Put the potatoes in a saucepan, cover with water, add a good pinch of salt, and bring to a boil. Cook until tender, drain well, and then dry in a clean dish cloth. Rub the potatoes through a fine strainer into a large bowl. Add the flour, egg, salt, pepper and nutmeg to taste. Mix together well, add the parsley, and beat to form a smooth dough.

With floured hands, roll the dough into long, ¾ inch diameter cylinders, then cut into ¾ inch pieces. Using a fork, make an indentation on each piece. Put the gnocchi on a floured tray until ready to cook.

Bring a large saucepan of salted water to a boil, then reduce to simmering, add the gnocchi, and poach gently for 3–4 minutes or until they rise to the surface of the water. Drain them well and keep warm in a buttered serving dish.

To make the sauce, boil ½ cup of water in a small saucepan, whisk in the pieces of cold butter a few at a time, then whisk in the blue cheese, and season to taste. Toss the gnocchi with the sauce and serve at once.

## Trenette with tuna and tomatoes

½ cup olive oil
2 cups flat mushrooms, cut into small cubes
1 tablespoon dried oregano
1 tablespoon fresh parsley, chopped
2 cups canned tomatoes, drained and roughly chopped
3 tablespoons tomato paste
sugar
1 cup canned tuna, drained and flaked
salt and freshly ground pepper
1 lb trenette pasta or spaghettini
freshly grated nutmeg

Heat half the olive oil in a skillet, add the cubed mushrooms, and cook over fairly high heat until lightly golden. Add the oregano and half the parsley.

Add the roughly chopped tomatoes, the tomato paste, and a pinch of sugar, and cook over low heat until the sauce thickens. Add the flaked tuna and gently stir into the sauce. Season to taste and stir in the remaining oil. Keep warm.

Cook the pasta in boiling salted water until al dente (just tender, but still firm to the bite). Drain well, return to the pan, and season with salt, pepper, and nutmeg. Put the pasta in a serving dish and pour over the tuna sauce. Sprinkle with the remaining chopped parsley and serve at once.

## Penne with spring vegetables and mint

2 strips of bacon, cut into small pieces
¾ cup frozen (or fresh) peas
¾ cup frozen (or fresh) fava beans, blanched and skinned
¾ cup young leeks, cut into ¼ inch slices
1½ cups chicken broth
5 tablespoons olive oil
2 oz butter
1 lb penne pasta
3 tablespoonsfresh mint leaves, chopped

Heat a heavy-bottomed saucepan, add the bacon, and sauté until the bacon releases its juices and becomes crisp. Remove from the pan and set aside.

Add the peas, beans, and leeks to the pan, cover with the broth, and cook until the vegetables are tender. Lift out the vegetables with a slotted spoon and keep warm.

Boil the broth over high heat until reduced to about ½ cup, then whisk in the oil and butter.

Meanwhile, cook the pasta in boiling water until al dente (just tender, but still firm to the bite). Drain well, then add to the sauce, and return the vegetables to the pan. Add the mint, toss together well, and serve at once, sprinkled with the crisp bacon.

## Crushed corn risotto with zucchini

4 oz butter
½ onion, finely chopped
1 cup arborio rice
2 cups chicken broth, hot
1 cup frozen or canned corn
5 tablespoons light cream
½ cup zucchini, sliced lengthwise into ribbons
3 tablespoons fresh mint, chopped
salt and freshly ground pepper

Heat 3 oz of the butter in a heavy-bottomed skillet, add the onion, and cook over low heat until tender. Add the rice and stir well to coat with butter. Add a little of the broth and stir until the liquid has been absorbed.

Keep adding the broth, a little at a time, stirring constantly, until the rice is tender but retains a little bite (about 20–25 minutes). Toward the end of the cooking time, add the broth in smaller quantities, and check whether the rice is done. The final consistency should be loose but not sloppy.

Meanwhile, put the corn and cream in a blender and blend to a coarse purée. Heat the remaining butter in a skillet, add the zucchini, and sauté until tender.

Add the corn purée to the risotto. Sprinkle the zucchini with the mint and a little salt and pepper, and gently stir them into the risotto. Serve at once.

## Chicken liver risotto

4 oz butter
½ onion, finely chopped
¼ teaspoon dried thyme
1 cup arborio rice
4 tablespoons dry white wine
3 cups chicken broth, hot
4 tablespoons vegetable oil
¾ lb chicken livers, cleaned and halved
½ cup madeira
½ cup heavy cream, lightly whipped

Melt 3 oz of the butter in a heavy-bottomed skillet, add the onion and thyme, and cook over low heat until softened but not browned. Add the rice and stir well to coat with the butter. Cook over low heat for 2 minutes until the rice becomes opaque.

Increase heat, pour in the wine, and cook for 4–5 minutes or until the wine has evaporated.

Add the broth, a little at a time, stirring constantly, adding more as it is absorbed, until about 2 cups of broth has been used and the rice is tender but retains a little bite (about 20–25 minutes).

Heat the oil and the remaining butter in a skillet, add the chicken livers, and cook over high heat to seal in their juices. Remove from the pan and keep warm. Add the madeira and the remaining 1 cup chicken broth to the pan and boil to reduce to a syrupy consistency.

To finish the risotto, beat in the cream and a little more butter, taste and adjust the seasoning if required. Divide the risotto between four serving dishes, top with the chicken livers and their sauce, and serve at once.

# **MAIN** COURSES

## Bourride of smoked haddock

2 oz butter
½ onion, chopped
1 garlic clove, crushed
1 cup leeks, finely chopped
1 carrot, cut into ¼ inch cubes
2½ cups potatoes, cut into ¼ inch cubes
1½ cups fish broth
1 lb smoked haddock
½ cup mayonnaise

Heat the butter in a saucepan, add the onion, garlic, and leeks, and cook over low heat for 5–8 minutes or until the vegetables are tender. Add the carrot and potato cubes, and cook for 5 minutes longer. Pour in the broth and bring to a boil, then reduce heat and simmer for 10 minutes.

Add the smoked haddock and cook for 5 minutes. Using a slotted spoon, remove the haddock and vegetables, and keep warm. Flake the fish into fairly large pieces.

Boil the broth over high heat to reduce it to 1 cup. Remove from heat and beat in the mayonnaise. Return to heat and bring to just below boiling point. Return the flaked fish and vegetables to the sauce, and serve hot.

## Kedgeree in filo purses

3 oz butter
½ onion, chopped
2 teaspoons curry paste
1 cup cooked rice (preferably basmati)
½ lb smoked haddock, cooked and flaked
3 eggs, hard-boiled and chopped
6 tablespoons heavy cream
salt and freshly ground black pepper
1 tablespoon fresh cilantro, chopped
8 sheets of filo pastry, 8 inches square

Heat half the butter in a large saucepan, add the onion, and cook over low heat until tender. Add the curry paste and stir to combine with the onion. Add the rice and mix well, then add the haddock and eggs, and stir in gently so that you do not break up the fish. Add the cream, season to taste, and transfer to a bowl. When cool, add the cilantro, and refrigerate for up to 1 hour.

Preheat the oven to 375°F.

Melt the remaining butter. Put 4 filo pastry squares on a work surface and brush with a little of the butter. Set another square of filo on top of each one and spoon a quarter of the kedgeree mixture into the center. Brush the edges of the pastry with a little more butter, then bring the sides up over the filling and pinch together to form purse shapes. Brush the outsides with butter, then bake for 12–15 minutes or until golden. Let cool slightly before serving.

## Baked sole with sardine tapenade

Canned sardines can be used if fresh are not available, but the result is not as good.

4 fresh fillets of sole, about ¼ lb each
salt and freshly ground pepper
8 small fresh fillets of sardines, boneless, finely chopped
1 onion, finely chopped
3 tablespoons black olives, finely chopped
1 tablespoon capers, drained and finely chopped
3 tablespoons fresh white breadcrumbs
½ cup olive oil
1 tablespoon maple syrup
1 tablespoon white wine vinegar
4 tablespoons mustard
1 tablespoon chives, chopped

Preheat the oven to 375°F.

Season the fillet of sole with a little salt and pepper. In a bowl, combine the sardines, onion, olives, capers, and breadcrumbs. Add salt and pepper with care: You should not need much salt.

Spread the mixture on the fillets of sole, roll up, and secure each fillet with a toothpick. Put on a baking sheet, spoon a little olive oil over each fillet, and bake for 8–10 minutes.

Meanwhile, heat the maple syrup and vinegar together in a small saucepan, then whisk in the mustard, olive oil, and chives.

Transfer the cooked fillets of sole to a serving dish and coat with the sauce; serve at once.

## Grey mullet in "acqua pazza"

Making mullet in "crazy water" (acqua pazza) is simplicity itself; I learned how when we hosted a culinary promotion with the hotel San Pietro from Positano in Italy.

4 fresh fillets of grey mullet
2 garlic cloves, thinly sliced
6 tablespoons olive oil
¼ teaspoon red pepper flakes
2 cups canned plum tomatoes, drained and chopped
3 tablespoons fresh parsley, chopped
1 teaspoon fresh or dried oregano
1 teaspoon anchovy extract (optional)
salt and freshly ground pepper

Remove all the bones from the fillets of grey mullet and set aside.

Put 2½ cups of water in a wide saucepan or deep skillet, and bring to a boil. Add the garlic, olive oil, and red pepper flakes, reduce heat and simmer for 10 minutes. Add the tomatoes, herbs, and anchovy extract, and simmer for 25 minutes longer; the mixture will reduce and thicken.

Season the fish with salt and pepper, and add to the pan. Simmer for 10 minutes or until cooked. Serve with steamed potatoes drizzled with olive oil.

# Baked cod with tomato and mustard sauce

This simple dish is elevated to gourmet status by serving it on a bed of creamy mashed potatoes to which you have added a generous spoonful of pesto sauce and a knob of butter. Sautéed zucchini are an ideal accompaniment.

4 fresh fillets of cod, about ¼ lb each, boneless, cleaned
1 oz butter
1 onion, finely chopped
1 tablespoon fennel seeds
pinch of mixed herbs
1 lb fresh tomatoes, skinned, deseeded, and roughly chopped
2 teaspoons English mustard
2 teaspoons brown sugar
salt and freshly ground pepper
pinch of cayenne pepper
1 tablespoon fresh parsley, chopped

Preheat the oven to 375°F. Put the fish in a lightly buttered oven-safe dish.

Heat the butter in a saucepan, add the onion, and sauté until tender. Add the fennel seeds, herbs, tomatoes, mustard and brown sugar. Mix well, then season to taste with salt, pepper and cayenne.

Pour the sauce over the fish and bake for 20–25 minutes. Sprinkle with fresh parsley and serve hot.

# Shanghai fishburgers with cumin and ginger ketchup

1 lb whiting or other fillet of white fish
1 tablespoon fresh root ginger, finely chopped
3 scallions, finely chopped
1 tablespoon fresh cilantro, chopped
¼ teaspoon red pepper flakes
1 tablespoon soy sauce
2 eggs, beaten
1 tablespoon cornstarch
salt and freshly ground pepper
5 tablespoons vegetable oil
2 hamburger buns
lettuce leaves, to serve

### For the cumin and ginger ketchup:
½ cup mayonnaise
1 tablespoon ketchup
¼ teaspoon ground cumin
¼ teaspoon fresh root ginger, chopped

Feel the fish to check there are no bones left. Mince the fish in a food processor and put in a bowl. Add the ginger, scallions, cilantro, red pepper flakes, and soy sauce, and stir to mix. Bind the mixture with the eggs and cornstarch, season lightly, then refrigerate for 1 hour.

Mix together all the ingredients for the ketchup in a small bowl.

Shape the chilled fish mixture into eight small burgers. Heat the oil in a skillet and sauté the fishburgers gently until golden, about 3–4 minutes on each side. Drain on paper towels.

Meanwhile, slice the buns in half and toast them, top with lettuce and the hot fishburgers, and serve at once, accompanied by the ketchup, and crisp, thin French fries.

## Fresh salt cod
## on herb-braised potatoes

4 fillets of cod, about ¼ lb each
1 tablespoon salt (preferably sea salt)
3 oz butter
1 onion, thinly sliced
freshly ground pepper
1 lb large potatoes
1 cup selection of fresh herbs (thyme, rosemary, parsley), chopped
1 cup chicken broth, boiling
½ cup olive oil

Put the fillets of fish in a shallow dish, sprinkle evenly with salt, and refrigerate overnight.

The next day, use 1 oz of the butter to grease an oven-safe serving dish. Preheat the oven to 375°F.

Heat 1 oz of the butter in a skillet and sauté the onion over low heat until golden. Season with salt and pepper.

Thinly slice the potatoes and layer them over the base of the buttered dish, season, and top with some of the onions; add another layer of potato slices, salt and pepper, more onion, and a final layer of potatoes. Sprinkle on the herbs. Dot the top layer of potatoes with the remaining butter, season with salt and pepper, and pour on the boiling broth. Bake for 50 minutes or until tender and golden.

Heat the olive oil in a skillet. Carefully wash and dry the fillets of cod, then sauté them in the oil for 1 minute on each side or until golden.

Put the fillets of cod on top of the potatoes, season lightly with salt and pepper, and return to the oven for 8–10 minutes. Serve hot.

## Cod tagine

4 fillets of cod (or other white fish), about ¼ lb each
⅔ cup vegetable oil
3 tablespoons ground cumin
2 teaspoons turmeric
1 onion, chopped
1 garlic clove, crushed
2 potatoes, cut into ½ inch cubes
2 carrots, cut into ½ inch cubes
⅔ cup pumpkin, cut into ½ inch cubes
1 teaspoon ground ginger
1 teaspoon ground cinnamon
2 cups canned cannellini beans
¼ cup prunes, soaked overnight and pitted

Marinate the cod with 5 tablespoons of the oil, the cumin, and turmeric, and refrigerate for 1 hour.

Preheat the oven to 400°F.

Heat the remaining oil in a large saucepan, add the onion and garlic, and cook over low heat until tender. Add the potatoes, carrots, and pumpkin, and sauté until golden, then add the ginger and cinnamon. Reduce heat and cook gently for 5 minutes.

Add the cannellini beans, prunes, and ½ cup of water and cook until the vegetables are tender. Taste and adjust the seasoning.

Put the fish on a baking sheet, brush with the marinade, and bake in the hot oven for 5–8 minutes or until cooked. Serve the fish on a warmed plate, surrounded by the tagine of vegetables, and accompanied by couscous.

## Broiled mackerel
## with sweet and sour rhubarb

Mackerel needs a sharp flavor to offset the oiliness of the
fish, such as this tangy rhubarb sauce.

5 tablespoons olive oil
1 cup canned tomatoes, drained and finely chopped
¾ lb fresh rhubarb, peeled and cut into small chunks
4 tablespoons brown sugar
3 tablespoons balsamic vinegar
salt and freshly ground pepper
pinch of ground cinnamon
pinch of ground ginger
1 tablespoon fresh cilantro, chopped
4 fresh mackerel, just under 1 lb each

Heat half the olive oil in a wide saucepan, add the tomatoes, and
simmer over low heat until they become thick and pulpy. Add the
rhubarb, brown sugar, and vinegar, and bring to a boil, then
reduce heat and cook gently for 8–10 minutes or until the sauce is
thick. Season to taste with salt, pepper, cinnamon, and ginger; you
may need to add a little more sugar if the rhubarb is very acidic.
Add the fresh cilantro to the sauce and keep warm.

Clean the mackerel, remove the fillets, and cut three small
incisions into the flesh on both sides. Season and brush them with
the remaining olive oil. Put under a hot broiler and cook for 5–6
minutes on each side, or until golden and crisp.

Serve the broiled mackerel with the rhubarb sauce,
accompanied by some sautéed eggplant slices.

## Braised chicken
## with anchovies and olives

8 chicken thighs
8 chicken drumsticks
4 tablespoons olive oil
salt and freshly ground pepper
2 garlic cloves, crushed
½ cup white wine
3 tablespoons balsamic vinegar
2 cups chicken broth
½ cup pitted black olives
4 anchovy fillets, rinsed to remove excess salt, drained, and
chopped

Cut three incisions in each piece of chicken. Heat the oil in a
flameproof casserole dish, add the seasoned chicken, and cook until
golden brown all over.

Add the garlic and stir to mix, then pour in the wine and
vinegar, and bring to a boil. Add the broth, olives, and anchovies.
Cover with a lid and simmer gently for 40–45 minutes until the
chicken is cooked and tender. Serve with buttered noodles.

## Bstila of chicken with sweet spices

3 oz butter
2 large chicken breasts
½ lb fresh chicken livers
salt and freshly ground pepper
1 small onion, chopped
½ teaspoon garlic, crushed
¼ teaspoon turmeric
¼ teaspoon ground ginger
¼ teaspoon ground cumin
¼ teaspoon ground allspice
a little chicken broth (optional)
1 egg
½ cup almonds, toasted
1 teaspoon ground cinnamon, plus extra for dusting
½ teaspoon sugar
½ cup cooked rice (preferably basmati)
3 tablespoons fresh cilantro or parsley, chopped
pinch of cayenne pepper
4 sheets of filo pastry, about 8 inches square
a little egg wash

Preheat the oven to 350°F.

Heat the butter in a skillet and sauté the lightly seasoned chicken breasts and livers over high heat until golden. Remove from the pan. Add the onion and garlic to the pan with the turmeric, ginger, cumin, and allspice, and cook for 1 minute to release their fragrance. Return the chicken breasts to the pan, half cover with broth or water, and bring to a boil. Reduce heat and simmer for 8 minutes. Add the livers and cook for 2–3 minutes longer. Remove the breasts and livers from the pan and cut them into ³⁄₄ inch cubes.

Boil the cooking liquid until it becomes syrupy in consistency. Let cool slightly, then whisk in the egg.

In a bowl, mix together the almonds, cinnamon, sugar, and cooked rice. Add the fresh herbs and cayenne pepper.

Put two sheets of filo pastry in a baking pan about 8 inches square. Brush with the sauce and egg mixture, then add the cubed chicken and livers. Top with the rice mixture, add the remaining sauce, then cover with the remaining filo pastry and tuck down the sides. Brush with egg wash and a light criss-cross dusting of cinnamon. Bake for 15–20 minutes or until golden. Serve hot.

## Broiled chicken wings on drunken black beans with chili verde

Instead of chicken wings, I also like to make this dish with lambs' kidneys or pork chops.

175 g (6 oz) black beans, cleaned and rinsed
1 garlic clove, crushed
1 tablespoon ground cumin
½ cup beer
4 tablespoons olive oil
salt and freshly ground pepper
8 chicken wings

**For the chili verde:**
½ green bell pepper, deseeded
1 green chili pepper, deseeded
4 tablespoons fresh cilantro, chopped
3 scallions, finely chopped
3 tablespoons white wine vinegar
½ teaspoon mustard
4 tablespoons olive oil

To make the chili verde, put the pepper, chili pepper, cilantro, and scallions in a blender and blend to a coarse purée. Transfer to a mixing bowl, add the vinegar, mustard, and oil. Season to taste. Let it reach room temperature to allow the flavors to infuse.

Put the black beans in a saucepan, cover with cold water, add the garlic and cumin, and bring to a boil. Reduce heat and simmer gently for about 1 hour or until tender. Add the beer toward the end of the cooking time. When the beans are cooked, the liquid will have reduced and formed a sauce around them. Add the olive oil and season to taste.

Broil the chicken wings under a hot broiler or over a barbecue. Arrange the wings on the black beans, drizzle over the chili verde and serve hot.

## Barbecue spice rub chicken

8 chicken thighs
8 chicken drumsticks

**For the spice rub:**
½ teaspoon salt
½ teaspoon sugar
½ teaspoon brown sugar
½ teaspoon red pepper flakes
½ teaspoon black pepper
½ teaspoon paprika
¼ teaspoon ground cumin
¼ teaspoon cayenne pepper

Combine all the ingredients for the spice rub in a large bowl. Using a sharp knife, cut three incisions in each piece of the chicken to allow the spices to permeate the flesh. Add the chicken to the dry ingredients and leave for 2 hours.

Cook on a barbecue or under a hot broiler. Serve with a yogurt and fresh herb dressing, and a leafy mixed salad.

## Turkey osso buco

1 large turkey leg, sawn through the bone into 2 inch "steaks"
4–5 tablespoons flour
salt and freshly ground pepper
4 tablespoons vegetable oil
1 oz butter
1 onion, finely chopped
2 carrots, cut into very small cubes
2 celery stalks, cut into very small cubes
½ leek, cut into very small cubes
1 garlic clove, crushed
1 tablespoon tomato paste
5 tablespoons dry white wine
3 tablespoons fresh orange juice
2 cups chicken broth

Preheat the oven to 325°F.

Remove the sinews and any small bones from the turkey steaks. Coat the turkey with flour, seasoned with salt and pepper. Heat the oil in a saucepan or flameproof casserole dish wide enough to take the turkey steaks in one layer. Brown the turkey on both sides in the hot oil, then remove, and set aside. Drain off any excess oil and add the butter to the pan.

Add the onion, carrots, celery, leek, and garlic, and cook over low heat until the vegetables are tender. Add the tomato paste and stir in. Cook over low heat for 2–3 minutes.

Add the wine and orange juice and boil for 3–4 minutes. Pour in the broth and return to a boil, adding a little salt and pepper.

Return the turkey to the pan, cover with a lid, and put in the oven for 1–1½ hours. Alternatively, simmer on the top of the stove.

Serve hot, with seasonal vegetables and, if you like, risotto, which is the classic accompaniment to osso buco.

## Spicy herb sausages in batter

My version of an old British favorite, "toad in the hole."

1 lb good-quality pork sausage meat
1 tablespoon fresh cilantro, chopped
1 tablespoon fresh oregano leaves
¼ teaspoon red pepper flakes
¼ teaspoon ground ginger
1 teaspoon mustard
4 scallions, finely chopped
salt and freshly ground pepper
¾ cup all-purpose flour
2 eggs
⅓ cup milk mixed with ¼ cup water
4 tablespoons vegetable oil
3 tablespoons caraway seeds (optional)

Put the sausage meat in a bowl and add the herbs, red pepper flakes, ginger, mustard, and scallions; mix in gently. Shape into eight small flat rounds and season with salt and pepper.

Sift the flour into a bowl, make a well in the center, add the eggs, and the milk and water, and mix to form a paste. Beat until smooth, then strain, and let stand for 30 minutes.

Preheat the oven to 400°F. Grease one large baking pan or eight individual molds with a little of the oil and put in the oven.

Heat the remaining oil in a skillet and sauté the sausage rounds for 1 minute on each side or until golden and sealed.

Pour the batter mix into the hot baking pan (or into the small molds), add the sausage rounds, and cook in the hot oven until risen and light in texture, about 30–35 minutes. If you like, sprinkle on the caraway seeds after about 20–25 minutes

## Daube of chicken with orange, cinnamon and rosemary

4 large fresh chicken legs
salt and freshly ground pepper
½ tablespoon ground cinnamon
4–5 tablespoons flour
4 tablespoons olive oil
1 oz butter
1 onion, finely chopped
1 garlic clove, crushed
1 tablespoon fresh rosemary, roughly chopped
½ cup red wine
2 cups chicken broth
8 oz can of tomatoes, chopped
¼ cup orange juice
sugar

Preheat the oven to 350°F.

Season the chicken legs with salt, pepper, and cinnamon. Dust them in the flour. Heat the oil in a flameproof casserole dish, add the chicken legs, and sauté until golden and sealed. Remove from the pan and set aside.

Drain off any excess fat, add the butter and the onion, and cook over low heat until tender. Add the garlic and rosemary, and cook for 1 minute. Pour in the red wine and bring to a boil, then add the broth and reduce heat.

Return the legs to the sauce, add the chopped tomatoes, orange juice, a good pinch of sugar, and a little salt and pepper. Cover with a lid and cook in the oven for 1 hour or until tender. Serve with polenta, beaten with plenty of butter.

## Braised shoulder of pork

If you can arrange your oven to take two casserole dishes, this satisfying dinner becomes even easier and more economical.

1¼ lb shoulder of pork, boneless
6 dried prunes, soaked overnight and drained
salt and freshly ground pepper
3 tablespoons vegetable oil
1 cup red wine
3½ cups chicken broth

### For the red cabbage:
1 red cabbage, about 1 lb
4 oz butter
5 tablespoons white wine vinegar
1 tablespoon sugar
4 tablespoons redcurrant jelly

Preheat the oven to 400°F. Take a knife and push a hole through the center of the pork. Fill the hole with the soaked prunes, pushing them in with your fingers. Season the pork with salt and pepper.

Heat the oil in flameproof casserole dish, and sauté the pork until golden and sealed on all sides.

Drain off the excess oil, then pour in the wine, and bring to a boil for 2 minutes. Pour in the broth, cover with a tight-fitting lid, and put in the hot oven for 1½ hours or until tender. During the cooking, baste the pork several times with the wine and broth.

Cut the cabbage into quarters, remove the central core and the faded outside leaves. Cut the cabbage into fine strips. Heat the butter in a saucepan or flameproof casserole dish, add the cabbage, vinegar, sugar, and 2 cups of water. Bring to a boil, then cover with a lid, and simmer for 45 minutes–1 hour. Alternatively, cook in the oven with the pork. When the cabbage is tender, remove the lid and boil to reduce any remaining liquid to a syrup. Add the redcurrant jelly to form a light glaze around the cabbage and season to taste.

To serve, slice the braised pork and serve on the cabbage, with some of the braising juices poured over. A tart apple sauce goes well with this dish.

## Chocolate chili pepper glazed pork

1½ lb pork belly, cut into strips
salt and freshly ground pepper
4 fresh red chili peppers, deseeded
3 tablespoons clear honey, warmed
2 oz unsweetened (bitter) chocolate, melted

Preheat the oven to 400°F. Season the pork, then roast in the hot oven for 30–35 minutes or until golden.

Meanwhile, in a blender, blend the chili peppers and the honey; pour into a bowl, add the melted chocolate, and mix well.

Remove the pork from the oven, drain on paper towels, brush with the chocolate glaze, and return to the oven for 10 minutes.

Serve on a bed of crisp mixed vegetables stir-fried with a little chopped fresh ginger.

## Korean-style barbecue lamb ribs

16 lamb ribs
salt and freshly ground pepper
5 tablespoons ketchup
½ cup soy sauce
½ tablespoon mustard
1 garlic clove, crushed
1 tablespoon sugar
1 tablespoon white wine vinegar
½ teaspoon ground ginger
3 teaspoons sesame seeds

Season the ribs with salt and pepper. Combine all the remaining ingredients together and coat the ribs in the mixture. Let marinate for up to 2 hours.

Put on a barbecue and broil for 20–25 minutes or until tender and slightly burnt on the edges. Alternatively, cook in a hot oven at 400°F.

## Persian koftas with pitta toasts

¾ lb lean ground lamb
¼ cup cooked rice
1 onion, finely chopped or shredded
1 teaspoon ground cinnamon
1 teaspoon ground cumin
salt and freshly ground pepper
2 eggs, beaten
4–5 tablespoons seasoned flour
3 oz butter
1 tablespoon olive oil
4 pita breads

### For the salad:

⅓ cup cucumber, cut into ½ inch cubes
1 red onion, cut into ½ inch cubes
½ garlic clove, crushed
4 tomatoes, deseeded, and cut into ½ inch cubes
5 tablespoons olive oil
juice of ½ lemon
3 tablespoons fresh cilantro, chopped

Put the ground lamb in a bowl, add the rice, onion, spices, salt, and pepper, and mix well. Add one of the eggs to bind the mixture. Wet your hands with water, then shape the lamb mixture into oval balls. Put in the refrigerator until ready to cook.

For the salad, mix all the ingredients together; season to taste.

When ready to cook, soak eight or more bamboo skewers in cold water for 30 minutes. Preheat the broiler or barbecue. Roll the meatballs in the seasoned flour, then in the remaining beaten egg. Thread them onto the skewers and broil, turning from time to time, until cooked and browned, about 15 minutes. Alternatively, heat the oil and butter in a skillet and sauté the meatballs until crisp and browned. Toast the pita breads and fill with the koftas and salad.

# VEGETARIAN DISHES

## Potato tortilla with rosemary and lemon

2½ cups new potatoes
salt and freshly ground pepper
1 garlic clove, halved
½ cup olive oil
1 tablespoon fresh rosemary, chopped
shredded zest of ½ lemon
5 eggs
2 scallions, finely chopped

Put the potatoes in a saucepan, cover with cold water, add salt, and bring to a boil. Reduce heat and cook until just tender. Drain and let cool.

When cold, cut the potatoes into thick slices. Rub an 8 inch omelet pan with the garlic clove. Heat 5 tablespoons of the oil, add the potato slices, and cook over low heat until golden. Add half the rosemary and the lemon zest and toss well to mix.

Beat the eggs in a bowl, season with salt and pepper, and add the scallions. Pour the mixture over the potatoes and cook over a fairly high heat for 1 minute or until the egg sets underneath. Carefully turn the omelet over and cook the other side. Sprinkle over the remaining rosemary and drizzle on the remaining oil; serve warm.

## Leeks Portuguese

½ cup olive oil
1 onion, finely sliced
1 garlic clove, crushed
1 lb young leeks, about 4 inches long, trimmed
¼ cup white wine
½ cup vegetable broth
6 coriander seeds, crushed
1 cup canned tomatoes, roughly chopped
sugar
salt and coarsely ground black pepper

Heat the olive oil in a wide saucepan, add the onion and garlic, and cook over low heat until tender. Add the leeks and cook for 2 minutes, then pour in the white wine. Bring to a boil and boil for 1 minute, then add the broth. Cover with a lid and simmer gently for 5–10 minutes or until the leeks are tender but not broken up. Using a slotted spoon, remove the leeks and set aside.

Add the coriander seeds and tomatoes to the cooking liquid and boil for 5–10 minutes or until thickened and slightly reduced. Season to taste with a pinch of sugar, salt, and pepper. Return the leeks to the liquid and let cool.

Serve at room temperature, sprinkled with coarsely ground black pepper.

## English muffin pizzas

A simple, convenient, and delicious alternative to a pizza base, with some of my favorite toppings listed below.

8 English muffins
olive oil

Halve the English muffins, brush with olive oil, and toast them lightly under a hot broiler, then add your choice of topping.

### Garlic mushroom

1 cup canned tomatoes, drained and chopped
3 tablespoons olive oil
1 garlic clove, crushed
1 cup button mushrooms, sliced
1 tablespoon capers
fresh or dried oregano
salt and freshly ground pepper

Put the tomatoes in a small saucepan and cook over high heat until they become quite thick and pulpy. Let cool.

Heat the oil in a skillet, add the garlic and mushrooms, and cook for 2 minutes. Add the capers and oregano, mix together, and season to taste. Spread the toasted English muffins with the tomato mixture, then top with the mushrooms. Put under a hot broiler for 3–4 minutes.

### Napoletana

8 fresh ripe tomatoes
3 tablespoons olive oil
1 onion, chopped
4–5 fresh sage leaves, chopped
1/3 cup black olives, pitted and chopped
2 anchovy fillets, drained and chopped (optional for vegetarians!)
Cheddar cheese, shredded

Cut the tomatoes into $1/4$ inch slices. Heat the oil in a small skillet, and add the onion, sage, olives, and anchovies, if using. Cook until the onion is tender.

Arrange the tomato slices on the toasted English muffins, spoon on the olive mixture, then top with shredded cheese. Put under a hot broiler for 3–4 minutes or until golden and bubbling.

### Blue cheese and walnut

5 tablespoons olive oil
1 red onion, thinly sliced
1/4 teaspoon dried sage
1 cup blue cheese (e.g., Gorgonzola)
3 tablespoons milk
3 tablespoons walnuts, toasted and roughly chopped

Heat 4 tablespoons of the oil in a saucepan over low heat, add the onion and sage, and cook until tender but not browned. Let cool.

Mash the cheese with the milk to make a smooth spread. Mix in the walnuts and the cooled onions. Chill.

Spread the mixture over the toasted English muffins and put under a hot broiler until golden.

### Chili bean

1 tablespoon vegetable oil
1/2 onion, chopped
1/4 teaspoon red pepper flakes
1 teaspoon ground cumin
1 tablespoon chopped fresh cilantro
2 cups canned black beans, chopped
1/2 avocado, sliced
3 tablespoons sour cream
3 tablespoons shredded Cheddar cheese

Heat the oil in a small skillet over low heat, add the onion, red pepper flakes, cumin, and cilantro, and cook until the onion is tender. Add the chopped black beans and continue cooking over low heat until the mixture is quite thick.

Spread the beans on the toasted English muffins and top with the avocado, sour cream, and shredded cheese.

## Lentil loaf

Wild mushrooms add a meaty flavor; they are expensive to buy, but if you pick your own they are a delicious addition.

1 oz butter
1 onion, finely chopped
1 garlic clove, crushed
1 cup button mushrooms (or wild mushrooms), chopped
1¾ cups brown lentils, cooked
1 cup oatmeal
¾ cup margarine
2 parsnips, coarsely shredded
salt and freshly ground pepper
cayenne pepper
freshly grated nutmeg

Heat the butter in a skillet, add the onion and garlic, and cook until tender Add the mushrooms and cook for 3–4 minutes. Add the cooked lentils and cook for a further 2–3 minutes. Transfer to a bowl and let cool.

Spread the oatmeal on a baking sheet and toast to a golden color, 5–8 minutes. Add the oatmeal to the lentil mixture, together with the margarine and the shredded parsnips. Season well with salt, pepper, cayenne, and nutmeg, and mix thoroughly.

Lay out a 10 inch square piece of buttered strong aluminum foil, and put the lentil mixture in the center. Roll up the aluminum foil and form a ball shape, twisting the ends to seal well.

Tie the aluminum foil ball in a damp dish cloth or piece of cheesecloth, and steam or poach in simmering water for 45 minutes.

To serve, let cool for 5 minutes, then carefully remove the cloth and aluminum foil, and slice the loaf into neat rounds. Serve on a bed of mashed potato purée and rutabaga..

## Cauliflower and potato curry with mint chutney

⅓ cup tablespoons vegetable oil
½ teaspoon turmeric
2 teaspoons ground cumin
1 tablespoon tomato paste
1 cauliflower, cut into flowerets
½ teaspoon red pepper flakes
1 cup canned tomatoes, drained and chopped
4 potatoes, cut into ¾ inch cubes
½ cup vegetable broth
1 teaspoon garam masala

### For the mint chutney:
½ cup fresh mint, chopped
2 small green chili pepper, deseeded and chopped
¼ onion, chopped
4 tablespoons fresh lemon juice

Heat the oil in a skillet, add the turmeric, cumin, and tomato paste, reduce heat and cook for 1–2 minutes. Add the cauliflower and stir to coat with the spices. Add the red pepper flakes, tomatoes and potatoes, stir well, and let cook for a further 4–5 minutes. Pour in the broth, bring to a boil, cover with a lid, and simmer gently until the vegetables are tender. Add the garam masala toward the end of cooking.

Serve with the chutney, made by placing all the ingredients in a blender, and blending to a coarse paste.

## Eggplant and basil pastitso

Use your favorite standby tomato-based pasta sauce–you will need about 3–4 cups.

1 large eggplant
salt and freshly ground pepper
2 cups macaroni
1 large jar of tomato sauce
$\frac{1}{2}$ cup olive oil

For the sauce:
$1\frac{1}{2}$ oz butter
$\frac{5}{8}$ cup flour
400 ml (14 fl oz) milk
5 tablespoons pesto sauce

Slice the eggplant into $\frac{1}{4}$ inch slices, spread on a tray, sprinkle with salt and let stand for 30 minutes.

Meanwhile, cook the macaroni in a large saucepan of boiling salted water until al dente (just tender but still firm to the bite), then drain in a colander. Heat the tomato sauce in a pan, add the drained macaroni, season to taste, and cook for 2 minutes longer to let the sauce flavor the pasta; set aside.

To make the sauce, melt the butter in a saucepan, stir in the flour, and cook over low heat for 1–2 minutes. Gradually add the milk and simmer, stirring all the time, for 2–3 minutes. Set aside.

Preheat the oven to 325°F. Rinse the eggplant slices well and pat dry. Brush with the olive oil and put in the oven until golden and tender.

Arrange half the eggplant slices in an oven-safe dish. Cover with half the macaroni mixture, then top with the remaining eggplant, and finish with a layer of macaroni. Pour over the white sauce, then spoon the pesto sauce in lines over the white sauce. Bake for 30–35 minutes or until golden; serve hot.

## Sambusak (Cheese and potato pasties)

This traditional dish from Syria and the Lebanon is usually made from a type of pizza dough; I use puff paste for convenience.

4 potatoes
salt and freshly ground pepper
freshly grated nutmeg
3–4 tablespoons cream cheese
1 tablespoon chopped fresh mint
$1\frac{1}{2}$ cups puff pastry
flour for rolling
vegetable oil for sautéing

Boil the potatoes until just tender. Drain well and let them become cold. When cold, cut them into $\frac{1}{2}$ inch cubes, add the salt and pepper, and a little nutmeg, and gently stir in the cheese and the mint, taking care not to break up the potatoes.

Roll out the puff paste thinly on a lightly floured surface and cut into rounds about 4 inches in diameter, using a pastry cutter or a small saucer as a guide. Put a tablespoon of the filling in the center of each puff paste round and fold the dough over the filling to make a half-moon shape.

Crimp the edges together to form small pasties and put in the refrigerator until required. To serve, sauté the pasties in hot oil until golden on both sides. Drain on paper towels and serve hot.

## Lentil moussaka tart

¾ cup lentils, soaked overnight
¾ cup vegetable oil
1 onion, finely chopped
1 garlic clove, crushed
1 teaspoon dried thyme
1 teaspoon ground allspice
3 tablespoons tomato paste
3 tablespoons flour
salt and freshly ground pepper
1 large eggplant
1 potato, thinly sliced
1 x 9 inch cooked shortcake pie shell

**For the cheese sauce:**
1 oz butter
¼ cup flour
1 cup milk
1 teaspoon mustard
½ cup cheese, shredded

Cook the lentils in about 2 cups water for 30–40 minutes or until tender. Drain and reserve the cooking liquid; you should have about 1 cup.

Heat 2 tablespoons of the oil in a saucepan, add the onion and garlic, and cook gently until tender. Increase heat, add the cooked lentils, the thyme, allspice, and tomato paste, and mix well. Cook for another 2 minutes. Add the flour and mix in well. Pour in the reserved lentil cooking liquid, a little at a time, to form a sauce around the lentils. Simmer for 10–15 minutes or until the sauce becomes quite thick. Season to taste and let cool.

Preheat the oven to 400°F. Make the cheese sauce, following the method on page 89, beating in the mustard and cheese at the end.

Slice the eggplant lengthwise into ½ inch thick slices. Sauté in the remaining oil until golden and tender. Drain on paper towels and season lightly. Parboil the potato slices for 2–3 minutes, drain, and pat dry. Fill each eggplant slice with lentil mixture, roll them up, and put them in the pie shell. Arrange the potato slices in overlapping rows over the eggplant to cover the pie. Pour the sauce over the potatoes, then put the pie into a hot oven for 15–20 minutes or until bubbling and golden.

## Winter vegetable goulash

5 tablespoons olive oil
1 small cauliflower, cut into flowerets
3 carrots, cut into ¼ inch slices
3 tablespoons butter
1 tablespoon caraway seeds
1 garlic clove, crushed
2 turnips, cut into ¼ inch slices
1 rutabaga, cut into ¼ inch slices
1 teaspoon paprika
1 tablespoon tomato paste
1 tablespoon flour
½ cup dry white wine
2 cups vegetable broth
2 zucchini, cut into ¼ inch slices
1 leek, cut into ¼ inch slices
salt and freshly ground pepper

Heat 4 tablespoons of oil in a heavy-bottomed saucepan, add the cauliflower and carrots, and cook gently for 2 minutes, without letting them brown.

Add the butter, caraway seeds, and garlic, and cook for 1 minute, then add the turnip and rutabaga. Sprinkle over the paprika to coat the vegetables. Stir in the tomato paste and flour, and cook over low heat for 2–3 minutes.

Pour in the wine, bring to a boil, and add the vegetable broth. Simmer until the vegetables are just cooked, but still slightly crisp.

Add the zucchini and leek, and cook for 2 minutes. Finally, add the remaining olive oil. Serve at once, with noodles or rice.

## Lentil koftas

½ cup lentils, soaked overnight
5 tablespoons vegetable oil
1 green chili pepper, deseeded and chopped
1 garlic clove, crushed
3 scallions, finely chopped
1 tablespoon ground cumin
½ tablespoon ground coriander
salt and freshly ground pepper
5 tablespoons rye flour (or all-purpose)

### For the raita:
1 celery stalk, cut into small cubes
½ cup cucumber, peeled and cut into small cubes
2 tomatoes, halved and cut into small cubes
⅓ cup plain yogurt
3 tablespoons fresh mint, chopped

Start making this dish the day before you want to serve it. Put the lentils in a saucepan, cover with cold water, and bring to a boil. Skim off any impurities from the surface of the water, then reduce heat, and cook for 30–40 minutes or until tender. Drain well.

Heat half the oil in a skillet, add the lentils, chili pepper, and garlic, and sauté until dry. Add the scallions, cumin, coriander, salt, and pepper, and cook for 2 minutes longer.

Add the flour, mix well, and cook over low heat for 3–4 minutes. Let cool, then refrigerate overnight.

To make the raita, mix all the ingredients together and chill. Alternatively, make the fruit raita on page 44.

To cook the koftas, heat the remaining oil in a skillet. Shape the lentil mixture into small ovals, and sauté gently until golden, about 2 minutes on each side. Serve hot, with the chilled raita.

## Savoy cabbage and parsnip jalousie

1 Savoy cabbage
2 oz butter
1 onion, thinly sliced
1 teaspoon sugar
1 teaspoon mustard
salt and freshly ground pepper
3½ cups parsnips, coarsely shredded
3 tablespoons caraway seeds
½ cup cooked brown rice
½ cup Cheddar cheese, shredded
2 eggs, beaten
1¾ cups puff paste
flour for rolling

Remove the outer leaves from the cabbage, blanch them in boiling salted water for 3–4 minutes, refresh under cold water, and then dry them well. Roughly shred the remainder of the cabbage.

Heat half the butter in a small skillet, add the onion and sugar, and cook until golden and caramelized. Remove from heat and let cool, then add the mustard, and season to taste.

Heat the remaining butter in a skillet, add the shredded cabbage, shredded parsnip, and 1 tablespoon caraway seeds, sauté for 3–4 minutes or until softened. Transfer to a bowl and let cool. Add the rice and cheese, and bind the mixture together with one of the eggs.

Preheat the oven to 375°F.

On a lightly floured surface, roll out the puff paste to measure about 8 by 12 inches. Arrange the outer cabbage leaves on the puff paste, leaving a 1 inch border around the edge. Top with the shredded cabbage mixture. Spoon the caramelized onions along the center of the filling.

Fold the puff paste over and press the edges to seal well. Very carefully lift the puff paste roll onto a baking sheet, turning the seam underneath. Brush all over with the remaining beaten egg, and decorate with any pastry trimmings. Brush again with egg, then sprinkle with remaining caraway seeds. Bake for 20–25 minutes or until cooked and golden brown.

# DESSERTS

## Sweet raisin fougasse

1 cake compressed yeast
4 cups flour, sifted
1 cyo sugar
3 tablespoons olive oil
1⅓ cups raisins, soaked in water
1 tablespoon clear honey

Dissolve the yeast in 1 cup warm water and leave for 5 minutes. Mix the flour with the sugar in a large bowl.

Add the oil to the yeast mixture, then add to the flour, and mix to form a smooth dough. Let rise in a warm, draught-free place for up to 1 hour or until doubled in size.

Pat the raisins dry on paper towels and work into the dough, then leave for another 30 minutes.

Preheat the oven to 400°F. Lightly grease a baking sheet. Form the dough into a flat oval shape, put on the baking sheet, and bake for about 30 minutes, until risen and golden. Brush with the honey as soon as it comes out of the oven. Let cool before serving with lots of heavy cream. Alternatively, this can be made in a loaf pan–and it makes great toast!

## Baked plums in red wine syrup

12 ripe medium-sized red or purple plums, halved
and pitted
1 cup sugar
½ cup red wine
juice and shredded zest of 1 orange
½ bay leaf
2 cloves

Preheat the oven to 300°F.

Put the plums in an oven-safe dish and sprinkle with the sugar. Put the wine in a saucepan with the orange juice and zest, bay leaf, cloves, and 3 tablespoons of water. Bring to a boil, boil for 2 minutes, then pour over the plums. Bake for 15–20 minutes or until the plums are tender and the cooking liquid has formed a syrup. (You may have to remove the plums and transfer the liquid to a saucepan to boil until reduced to a coating consistency.)

Serve warm or cold. This is excellent with vanilla ice cream.

## Cinnamon baked apples "en papillote"

These apples formed part of the original $2 menu for four that sparked off the idea for this book.

3 oz butter
⅓ cup sugar
½ teaspoon ground cinnamon
2 drops of vanilla extract
juice of ½ orange
4 ripe Golden Delicious apples

Preheat the oven to 375° F.

Melt the butter in a saucepan, add the sugar, cinnamon, vanilla extract, orange juice, and 5 tablespoons of water, and boil until caramelized to a light, sticky syrup.

Core the apples with an apple corer or a melon baller, and make a few incisions in the skins to prevent the apples from bursting while they are cooking.

Butter a sheet of aluminum foil about 15 inches square, and put on a baking sheet (the edges will be overhanging at this stage). Lay the apples on the aluminum foil, leaving a gap of about $1\frac{1}{2}$ inches between them. Brush the syrup over the apples, bring the aluminum foil up to the top, and seal together. Put in the oven and bake for 20–25 minutes or until the apples are tender.

Bring the aluminum foil parcel to the table and then undo the foil to release the aroma. Serve the apples with the cooking juices poured over them.

## Double orange dessert

½ cup milk
½ cup sugar
½ teaspoon vanilla extract
juice and shredded zest of 1 orange
1½ oz butter
¾ cup flour
3 eggs, separated
½ cup coarse orange marmalade

Preheat the oven to 350°F. Lightly butter four individual ramekin or custard cups (or tea cups), about $\frac{1}{2}$ cup each.

Bring the milk to a boil with half the sugar, the vanilla extract, and orange zest, then let cool slightly.

In another saucepan, melt the butter and stir in the flour to form a smooth paste. Cook over low heat for about 1 minute, stirring constantly, then gradually pour in the warm milk, beating well until smooth. Add the orange juice and cook the sauce over low heat for 5–8 minutes, then let cool slightly before beating in the egg yolks.

Whisk the whites until stiff, then fold in the remaining sugar. Beat half the whites into the sauce, then carefully fold the sauce into the remaining whites until evenly combined. Divide the mixture between the buttered cups, but do not overfill them: They should be about two-thirds full.

Put the cups in a roasting pan with about $\frac{3}{4}$ inch hot water in the bottom and cook for 20 minutes or until risen and set.

Meanwhile, heat the marmalade in a small saucepan with $\frac{1}{2}$ cup of water to form a sauce.

Turn the desserts out onto warmed serving plates, and serve at once, with the sauce poured over them. For an elegant presentation, decorate with orange segments and sprigs of mint.

## Apple bread and butter sponge pudding

5 tablespoons melted butter
4 slices of white bread (or 4 white crusty rolls)
2 Golden Delicious apples, cored and thinly sliced
¾ cup raisins
2 cups milk
½ teaspoon vanilla extract
4 eggs
5 tablespoons sugar
3 tablespoons apricot jam, warmed
confectioner's sugar to dust

Preheat the oven to 325°F. Butter an oven-safe dish.

Butter the bread, then cut each slice into four triangles; if using rolls, cut them into ¼ inch thick slices. Arrange the bread in the dish, overlapping neatly, with the thinly sliced apple between the slices of bread. Sprinkle over the raisins and set aside.

Bring the milk to a boil with the vanilla extract.

In a bowl, beat the eggs with the sugar, then carefully pour on the hot milk, a little at a time, whisking continuously until the mixture forms a smooth custard. Strain the custard, then pour it over the bread.

Put the dish in a roasting pan containing about 1 inch of boiling water, and bake for 40 minutes or until just firm to the touch. Remove from the oven and let cool slightly. Brush with the apricot jam. Just before serving, dust with a little confectioner's sugar.

## Prune and almond frittata

⅔ cup dried prunes, pits removed, soaked overnight in cold tea
2 oz butter
5 tablespoons brandy (optional luxury)
6 eggs, beaten
5 tablespoons sugar
5 tablespoons ground almonds
3 tablespoons almond flakes
confectioner's sugar to glaze

Preheat the broiler.

Cut the prunes into quarters and pat them dry. Heat the butter in an omelet pan about 6 inches in diameter. Add the prunes and heat through for 1 minute. Add the brandy, if using, and ignite. Shake the pan until the flames die down.

In a bowl, beat the eggs with the sugar and ground almonds. Pour the egg mixture onto the prunes, and stir gently with a fork over fairly high heat until lightly set. Sprinkle over the almond flakes, and dust with plenty of confectioner's sugar. Put the pan under the hot broiler until the confectioner's sugar forms a golden glaze.

Invert onto a warmed serving plate, dust with a little more confectioner's sugar, and serve at once, with a big spoonful of heavy cream.

## Cinnamon and lemon fritters

½ cup milk
juice and shredded zest of 1 lemon
4 tablespoons butter
¼ teaspoon salt
1 cup plus 2 tablespoons sugar
¾ cup all-purpose flour, sifted
2 eggs
vegetable oil for deep-fat frying
1 teaspoon ground cinnamon

Put the milk, lemon zest, butter, salt, and half the sugar in a saucepan, and bring to a boil. Add the flour all at once and beat to a smooth paste, using a wooden spoon. Reduce heat and continue beating until the dough leaves the sides of the pan clean. Let cool slightly, then add the eggs one at a time, beating well after each addition.

Heat the oil for deep-fat frying to 350°F (until a cube of bread browns in 30 seconds).

Carefully drop teaspoonfuls of the mixture into the hot oil and cook for 4–5 minutes until golden. It is best not to cook too many spoonfuls in each batch. Drain the fritters on paper towels. Mix the remaining sugar with the cinnamon and roll the hot fritters in the cinnamon sugar. Serve hot with vanilla ice cream.

## Caramelized bananas with coconut fried ice cream

2 cups vanilla ice cream
1 egg, beaten
¾ cup flour, sifted
5 tablespoons sweetened, shredded coconut
5 tablespoons fresh white breadcrumbs
4 bananas
½ cup maple syrup
½ cup orange juice
3 tablespoons fresh lemon juice
3 tablespoons rum (optional luxury)
vegetable oil for deep-fat frying

Prepare the ice cream the day before you want to serve this dish. Using an ice cream scoop, scoop four balls of ice cream, and put in the freezer on a sheet of aluminum foil. Prepare a thick batter by beating together the egg, flour, and 5–6 tablespoons water. Mix the sweetened, shredded coconut with the breadcrumbs in a shallow dish. Dip the ice cream balls in the batter, then roll them in the coconut mixture to coat them thickly and evenly. Return to the freezer and freeze overnight.

When required, peel the bananas and cut each one in half lengthwise. Heat the maple syrup, orange and lemon juice, and rum, if using, in a skillet over moderate heat. Add the bananas and cook for 3–4 minutes, adding a little water if necessary, so that the bananas are caramelized, warmed through, and surrounded by light syrup.

Heat the oil until a cube of bread browns in 30 seconds. Cook the ice cream balls until they are just golden. Serve at once, with the bananas and the caramelized juices.

## Clafoutis of plums and raisins

2 eggs
1 egg yolk
¼ cup caster sugar
⅓ cup flour
½ cup milk
2 drops of vanilla extract
1½ oz butter, melted
1 lb fresh ripe plums, halved, pitted, and cut into pieces
4–5 tablespoons brown sugar
confectioner's sugar to dust

Preheat the oven to 350°F.

Put the eggs, egg yolk, and caster sugar in a bowl, and beat together until light. Gradually sift in the flour and beat to obtain a smooth batter. Add the milk, the vanilla extract, and 1 oz of the melted butter, and beat again until smooth.

Heat the remaining butter in a heatproof dish, about 8 x 5 inches. Add the plums and brown sugar, and cook for 1 minute, then pour on the batter.

Put in the oven and cook until golden and set, yet still light and soft inside. Dust with confectioner's sugar and serve with heavy cream.

## Rhubarb and polenta tart

½ cup sugar
¾ lb rhubarb, peeled and cut into 2 inch lengths
5 tablespoons flour
5 tablespoons polenta
5 tablespoons soft brown sugar
½ teaspoon ground cinnamon
2 oz cold butter, cut into small pieces
1 x 9 inch pie crust

Preheat the oven to 350°F.

Put the sugar in a saucepan with ½ cup of water, bring to a boil, and boil for 2 minutes. Add the rhubarb and simmer for 2 minutes longer. Drain and set aside.

Put the flour, polenta, brown sugar, cinnamon, and butter in a blender or food processor, and pulse until the mixture resembles coarse sand.

Put the drained rhubarb in the pie crust, and sprinkle over the polenta crumble mixture. Put in the oven for about 20 minutes or until the topping is golden and crisp.

## Baked fruit kebabs with chocolate couscous

2 oranges

2 bananas

1 ripe pear

4 pitted prunes, soaked and halved

5 tablespoons sugar

3 tablespoons rum

### For the couscous:

1 cup milk

3 tablespoons sugar

½ tablespoon sweetened cocoa powder

½ cup couscous

3 tablespoons rum (optional luxury)

For the couscous, heat the milk and sugar in a small saucepan, add the cocoa, stir well, and bring to a boil. Put the couscous in a bowl, pour over the chocolate milk, stir well, then cover and let stand for 5–8 minutes. Separate the grains of couscous with a fork, cover, and let stand for another 5 minutes. Stir once again, add the rum, if using, and refrigerate.

Soak four bamboo skewers in cold water for about 30 minutes. Preheat the oven to 450°F.

Peel the oranges, bananas, and pear. Cut each banana into eight thick slices. Cut the oranges into quarters, and cut the pear in half, remove the core, then cut into quarters.

Thread the fruit onto the skewers, with the prune halves at each end of the skewers. Put the fruit skewers in a shallow, oven-safe dish.

Boil the sugar with 3 tablespoons of water for 5 minutes, then pour over the fruit skewers. Add the rum, if using, and bake in a hot oven for 5 minutes, basting from time to time.

Serve the chilled couscous on a platter, topped with the hot fruit kebabs. Spoon over a little of the hot syrup from the baking dish. Vanilla ice cream or fruit sorbet are good accompaniments.

## Coffee risotto

1 tablespoon instant coffee powder

shredded zest and juice of ½ orange

½ cup arborio rice

2 cups milk

2 drops of vanilla extract

½ cup sugar

1 oz butter

¾ cup heavy cream

3 tablespoons rum (optional)

Put the coffee and orange juice in a saucepan with ½ cup of water and bring to a boil. Remove from heat, add the rice, and let soak for 5 minutes.

Return the pan to heat and add the milk and vanilla extract. Cook over low heat until rice is tender, but still slightly firm to the bite.

Remove from heat, add sugar, orange zest, butter, cream, and rum (if using), stir through gently, and serve at once.

## Corn ice cream
## with summer berry compote

3 egg yolks
1 egg
²/₃ cup sugar
1¾ cups milk
1 cup heavy cream
³/₄ cup canned corn, puréed

**For the compote:**
4 tablespoons sugar
3 cups mixed berries (strawberries, blackberries, raspberries)
sprigs of mint to decorate

To make the ice cream, whisk the egg yolks, egg, and sugar until pale in color and doubled in volume. Boil the milk and cream together, then let cool slightly. Pour the milk, a little at a time, onto the egg mixture, stirring all the time. Add the puréed corn and strain through a strainer.

Return the mixture to the saucepan and cook over low heat, stirring constantly, until the mixture thickens enough to coat the back of a spoon (do not let it boil.)

Cool the mixture quickly. When cold, pour into an ice cream machine, and freeze. When the ice cream is set, transfer it to a plastic container, and put in the freezer.

To make the compote, put the sugar in a saucepan with 4 tablespoons of water, bring to a boil, add the berries, and remove from heat. Cover and let cool completely.

Before serving, let the ice cream soften a little at room temperature. Spoon the fruit compote onto individual soup plates. Top with a ball of the corn ice cream and decorate with sprigs of mint.

## Banana "Wednesday"

**Why save a sundae for Sunday?**

4 bananas
3 tablespoons soft brown sugar
4 tablespoons heavy cream
1½ oz unsalted butter
¼ teaspoon vanilla extract
4 scoops of chocolate ice cream
1 tablespoon almonds flakes
sprigs of mint to decorate

Preheat the oven to 400°F.

Put the bananas on a baking sheet and bake for 5–8 minutes or until they are warmed through but not soft.

Meanwhile, prepare the sauce. Put the sugar, cream, butter, and vanilla extract in a heavy-bottomed saucepan and cook, stirringm, for 3–5 minutes or until the mixture turns a light caramel color.

Peel the bananas and cut them in half lengthwise or into slices.

Put the chocolate ice cream in individual dishes, top with the roasted bananas, and pour over the caramel sauce. Sprinkle over the toasted almonds and decorate with the mint.

## Asian toffee rice dessert

2 oz butter
½ cup light brown sugar
¼ teaspoon ground cinnamon
10 cardamom pods, shelled and seeds crushed
pinch of freshly grated nutmeg
½ cup ground rice (semolina)
3½ cups milk
¼ cup golden raisins

Heat the butter and sugar together in a saucepan until slightly caramelized. Add the spices and the rice, and stir well.

Add the milk, a little at a time, stirring well to prevent lumps from forming. When all the milk has been added, reduce heat, add the golden raisins, and cook over low heat for about 25 minutes. If the custard becomes too thick, add a little more milk. Serve hot or cold. I particularly like this dessert served cold with a compote of apricots, topped with toasted almonds.

## Poached pears
## in espresso-cardamom syrup

4 firm but ripe dessert pears
1 cup strong coffee (espresso)
⅔ cup sugar
6 cardamom pods, crushed
juice and shredded zest of ½ lemon
3 tablespoons almonds flakes, toasted
sprigs of mint to decorate

Using a potato peeler, peel the pears neatly, leaving the stalks intact and keeping the shape of the pear. Cut a little off the base of each pear to help it remain upright while it is poaching.

Choose a saucepan that will hold the four pears upright side by side. Put the coffee, sugar, ⅔ cup of water, cardamom, and the the lemon juice and zest in the pan and bring to a boil, stirring until the sugar has dissolved. Add the pears, cover the pan, reduce heat, and simmer for about 20–25 minutes or until the pears are tender but still retaining their shape.

Using a slotted spoon, remove the pears from the syrup, and transfer to a bowl. Boil the syrup rapidly until reduced to about ½ cup. Let cool, then pour the syrup over the pears, and put in the refrigerator for up to 4 hours, to chill thoroughly.

Serve the pears with the coffee syrup, sprinkle over the toasted almonds, and decorate with the mint. Serve with heavy cream or vanilla yogurt.

## Lemonade granita
## with raspberry sauce

6 juicy lemons
²/₃ cup sugar
1½ cups frozen raspberries (or fresh, in season)
1 tablespoon caster sugar
raspberries and sprigs of mint to decorate

Finely grate the zest of one of the lemons. Squeeze the juice from all the lemons. Put the sugar, 1¹/₂ cups of water, and the lemon zest in a saucepan, bring to a boil, reduce heat, and simmer until the sugar has dissolved. Add the lemon juice and let cool.

Pour the liquid into a shallow dish (preferably stainless steel) approximately 6 inches square, and put in the freezer.

After 30 minutes or so the liquid will start to set on the surface and around the edge of the dish. Using a fork, scrape it until the loose crystals of ice are evenly distributed. Return to the freezer for another 30 minutes. Repeat the scraping process twice more.

Put the raspberries in a blender with the caster sugar and blend to a purée. Rub through a strainer to remove any seeds.

To serve, scoop the lemon granita into individual glasses, pour over the raspberry sauce, and decorate with raspberries and mint.

## Blackberry ice cream soda

Some of you may remember enjoying ice cream sodas when you were young. Here is a real taste of nostalgia and late-summer simplicity.

2½ cups fresh blackberries
a little caster sugar
4 scoops of vanilla ice cream
1 cup cream soda

Sweeten the blackberries with a little sugar if required. Divide the berries between four tall glasses and top with the ice cream. Pour over the soda and serve immediately, while it is still bubbling.

# INDEX

# Acknowledgements

A million thanks to my wife, Anita, whose help and patience behind the scenes has been truly invaluable, and to my children Lee, Ryan, Lauren, and Rosie, to whom this book is dedicated.

I would also very much like to thank the following people for their invaluable contributions to this book:

Bridget Sargeson and Jane Suthering, food stylists, and Julian Marshall, my executive sous-chef, who between them prepared the dishes for photography; I thank them all immensely.

Photographer Philip Wilkins, for the care and true professionalism that went into each photograph, which is evident in the final product.

Sue Russell, for her beautiful photographic props and materials.

All at Weidenfeld & Nicolson, particularly Nick Clark and Maggie Ramsay, and Editorial Director Susan Haynes, for her belief and interest in the idea.

Geoffrey Gelardi, Managing Director at the Lanesborough, for his continuing support and encouragement in my new projects.

Finally, I must not forget to thank Simon Hinde, Consumer Affairs Correspondent for the *Sunday Times,* who set the challenge in 1995 that set the whole idea of this book in motion.